The student's writing guide
for the arts and social sciences

GORDON TAYLOR

Language and Learning Unit
Faculty of Arts, Monash University

CAMBRIDGE
UNIVERSITY PRESS

Published by the Press Syndicate of the University of Cambridge
The Pitt Building, Trumpington Street, Cambridge CB2 1RP
40 West 20th Street, New York NY 10011-4211, USA
10 Stamford Road, Oakleigh, Melbourne 3166, Australia.

First published 1989
Reprinted 1990, 1992, 1994

Printed in Great Britain by the Bath Press, Avon

British Library cataloguing in publication data

Taylor, Gordon
The student's writing guide
for the arts and social sciences.
1. Essays. Composition – Manuals
I. Title
808.4

Library of Congress cataloguing in publication data

Taylor, Gordon.
The student's writing guide
for the arts and
social sciences / Gordon Taylor.
        p.   cm.
Bibliography: p.
Includes index.
ISBN 0 521 36005 6.   ISBN 0 521 36905 3 (pbk)
1. English language – Rhetoric.
2. Report writing.
3. Arts – Authorship.
4. Social sciences – Authorship.
I. Title.
PE1478.T38 1988
808'.042 – dc19   88 17040 CIP

ISBN 0 521 36005 6 hard covers
ISBN 0 521 36905 3 paperback

CE

For
KASONDE, SUSAN
and JEREMY

Contents

vii

Contents

Contents

x

Preface

This book has grown out of a writing course I have taught for some years to students of the arts and social sciences. In both I have tried to emphasise the close connections between writing in these disciplines and grappling with the problems of knowledge and understanding they present. Writing is not merely a skill we employ to record our knowledge, but the very moment at which we confront what learning and understanding are all about. So, while the reader will surely find plenty of guidance on the practical issues that arise in writing an academic essay, a search in these pages for simplified techniques that side-step the very taxing work of coming to terms with knowledge and method in these disciplines will be fruitless. My project has been to clear paths, not to indicate short cuts.

It has been my experience that many students' writing problems arise from uncertainty about what it is they are trying to say and what it is they have to do. So far as is possible in a general work of this kind, I have attempted to establish, in a variety of representative disciplines, some of the connections between issues of content and the forms of language in which the content can be realised. I am conscious that there are arts and social science disciplines which have not received extended treatment in the examples. But I trust that in concentrating attention on some of the most important things that we *do* with language in academic studies I have been able to direct readers to the kind of thing to look for in the particular disciplines they are studying.

The book is divided into three parts. I suggest the chapters of Parts I and II be read through at least once in the order presented. In this way the student will get a general idea of how to approach the writing of an academic essay. Not everybody approaches writing and learning in quite the same fashion, so it is important that the suggestions in Parts I and II be interpreted in a way that works best for the individual reader. The chapters of Part III contain in many instances extensions of themes introduced earlier, but they can also be read as more or less self-contained introductions to particular problems in the use of language. For the most part, grammatical and other details of language use are dealt with not in the manner of the conventional guides to usage but as they arise in those contexts of meaning we concentrate on as we write. It will therefore be necessary to make good use of the index. Part III is not a comprehensive guide to the language of academic discourse. I have chosen to treat only those features of language which students often question me about, those which in my estimation cause most trouble, and those which (spelling apart) tutors most regularly draw attention to in their marking of essays.

The book has been some time in the gestation. To John Clanchy, Brigid Ballard and Elaine Barry I owe many thanks for their encouragement and for commenting on drafts which they have now probably forgotten. I. W. Mabbett helped me greatly to clarify my thinking on some of the material in chapter 3, and the readers of the Cambridge University Press have made this a better book than it would otherwise have been. My students have contributed much: not only have they let me use their work, they have pushed me to understand certain things about writing I would never have gleaned elsewhere. But it is on the person who, as the psalmist says, can 'alway keep judgement' and who has believed in this book when I didn't myself that I have depended most – my wife Angela.

Sources of extracts
used in the text

Dwight Bolinger, *Language – the Loaded Weapon*. London and New York: Longman, 1980

Crane Brinton, *The Anatomy of Revolution*, revised and expanded edn. New York: Vintage Books (Random House, Alfred A. Knopf), 1965

R. N. Campbell and R. J. Wales, 'Comparative structures in English'. *Journal of Linguistics*, 5:2 (1969), pp. 215–51

E. H. Carr, *What is History?* Harmondsworth: Penguin, 1964

Manning Clark, *A Discovery of Australia*. The Boyer Lectures. Sydney: Australian Broadcasting Corporation, 1976

A. C. Ewing, *A Short Commentary on Kant's 'Critique of Pure Reason'*. Chicago: University of Chicago Press, 1938

Immanuel Kant, *Critique of Pure Reason*, trans. F. Max Müller. New York: Anchor Books (Doubleday), 1966

F. R. Karl and L. Davies (eds.) *The Collected Letters of Joseph Conrad*. Cambridge: Cambridge University Press, 1983

Norman Kemp Smith, *A Commentary to Kant's 'Critique of Pure Reason'*, 2nd edn. New York: Humanities Press, 1962

Walter Nash, *Designs in Prose*. London: Longman, 1980

A. R. Radcliffe-Brown and D. Forde (eds.) *African Systems of Kinship and Marriage*. London: Oxford University Press, 1950

W. G. Runciman, 'What is structuralism?' In Alan Ryan (ed.) *The Philosophy of Social Explanation*. London: Oxford University Press, 1973

Sources of extracts

George H. Sabine, *A History of Political Theory*, 3rd edn. London: George G. Harrap, 1963

C. R. Seligman, G. R. Tucker and W. E. Lambert, 'The effects of speech style and other attributes on teachers' attitudes towards pupils'. *Language in Society*, 1:1 (1972), pp. 131–42

T. D. Weldon, *Kant's 'Critique of Pure Reason'*, 2nd edn. Oxford: Clarendon Press, 1958

John B. Whittow, *The Penguin Dictionary of Physical Geography*. London: A. Lane, 1984

John M. Wilding, *Perception, From Sense to Object*. London: Hutchinson, 1982

1
Introduction

How do I know what I think till I
see what I say.

E. M. FORSTER

How do I know what I'll say till I see
what I think.

ANON.

1 The main elements in academic writing

If we are to write well we need to know (as well as we can) what
we are talking about. In order to find out what, precisely, we are
talking about we need to write. Pushing ourselves to write will
often reveal that we know more about a subject than we at first
supposed; it should just as often reveal large gaps in our
understanding of matters we thought ourselves fairly sure of. In
writing we bring knowledge into being, we record and preserve
it. Writing is the seed, the fruit and the pickle of our understanding.

Most people in the English-speaking world used to think that
the student's and scholar's mind is an empty bucket to be filled by
books, lectures and tutorials. Nowadays physiologists and
psychologists tell us that the brain doesn't work in this passive,
accepting matter. On the contrary, to learn and to write is, first,
to make sense for ourselves of our new experience in terms of our
old. So you need to be aware at the outset that, even to subjects
you have never studied before, you can bring certain preconcep-
tions, even prejudices, a certain amount of disjointed knowledge, and a certain facility with language – all of which can get
you started. The most baffling of essay topics can soon yield
some meaning if you take the initiative and begin to ASK
QUESTIONS – of yourself, of the essay topic, of your books and

lectures, of the school or department for whom you are writing the essay. To think of yourself as an active enquirer, rather than as a mere receptacle of ideas and knowledge or as a passive medium by which they are transmitted from your books to your essays, is essential to good essay-writing. Good academic writing actually *creates* new knowledge and new meaning.

Now there is no single TECHNIQUE by which this can be achieved. Rather, there seem to be four elements whose relationships with one another need to be balanced: the writer, the object of the analysis or discussion (the content), the reader, and the formal properties of the language itself. Not everybody will balance these elements in quite the same way; and this is as it should be, since there is no such thing as a uniform, ideal academic English. Getting the balance right will depend partly on how you, the writer, respond in particular circumstances and partly on those traditions of expression and scholarship which grow up within certain disciplines, schools of thought within disciplines and within particular college and university departments.

These four elements of the writing situation – writer, subject matter, reader and the forms of language – are reflected in four main characteristics of a piece of written language itself. They must all be handled together in the act of writing. Their competing claims to attention are resolved in the choice of one word in preference to another, in the structuring of a sentence, in the placing of an emphasis in the paragraph, and so on. The four characteristics are these:

- Your own point of view must emerge, not as a mere opinion but as a JUSTIFIED JUDGEMENT.
- You need to treat your subject matter as comprehensively and as precisely as the essay topic demands. You must read widely and from the range of information and ideas create a unified view. You must read carefully and do your best to make your language clarify the information and ideas you find in your books.
- You must present your work in the appropriate fashion for

academic readers. This means that you will have to learn certain CONVENTIONS of academic writing which are, at times, quite different from those you may be used to.

- Finally, the text of your essay needs to forge a coherent unity from the many diverse elements of language and thought that go to make it. It is in many of the details of your text that your purpose is realised. An essay is not merely a vehicle for ideas, but is itself (whatever the discipline) a piece of literature.

It is best to conceive of essay-writing as entering into a debate. You need to work out what your own answer to the essay question might be. You need to debate it with the books and other sources of information and ideas you use. And then you need to convey the results of this engagement clearly to your reader, bearing in mind that the reader – because of what he or she already knows – needs to be convinced that your own answer is a reasonable one. Fundamental to this whole process is your use of language. This is the main evidence your tutors have to go on in making their assessment of your essay – just as you have mainly the evidence of language in your books to judge the usefulness and value of their authors' work to you.

The aim of this book is to show you how to fit together the elements introduced above, and to help you participate successfully in written academic debate. But first we shall examine each of our elements separately in a little more detail, beginning with that bane of all writers' lives – 'writer's block'.

2 You and your writing task

For most people writing is an extremely difficult task if they are trying to grapple in their language with new ideas and new ways of looking at them. Sitting down to write can be an agonising experience, which doesn't necessarily get easier with the passage of time and the accumulation of experience. For this reason you need to reflect upon and analyse your own reactions to the task of writing. That is to say, the task will become more manageable if you learn how to cope with your own particular ways of avoiding or putting off the moment when you must set pen to paper.

First of all, it is as well to be aware that this fear of putting pen to paper is very widespread, and not only amongst students. The novelist Joseph Conrad describes his fear and lack of confidence in quite harrowing terms:

> I am not more vile than my neighbours but this disbelief in oneself is like a taint that spreads on everything one comes in contact with; on men, on things – on the very air one breathes. That's why one sometimes wishes to be a stone-breaker. There's no doubt about breaking a stone. But there's doubt, fear – a black horror, in every page one writes.

Just as the fear of writing is widely shared, even amongst successful writers, so are the frustrations of confronting the writing pad. Bertrand Russell, one of the most accomplished and prolific of scholars and writers, has described in his auto-biography how he would sit for days on end staring at his paper when he was working on the *Principia Mathematica*: 'it seemed quite likely that the whole of the rest of my life might be consumed in looking at that blank sheet of paper'. Russell had no 'method' to which he could turn to get him started.

If we could hazard a generalisation, it is this. Some degree of routine, of regular writing times alone by oneself, seems to be one ingredient that many writers find necessary. Even if nothing happens, it might be a good idea to sit out an allotted period before the paper rather than go rushing off to the library or your friends in search of inspiration. Most books on study skills recommend drawing up some kind of timetable for your work, and even the most arbitrary of rules (like 500 words a day, even if all 500 have later to be scrapped or rewritten) can serve a useful purpose. Many writers work like this. Others have more specific routines. The economist John Maynard Keynes worked in bed until lunch-time. Graham Greene, the novelist, gets up each morning and starts to write straightaway, before shaving, dressing or breakfasting. The solutions are as endless as the personalities, the family circumstances, the opportunities and the 'lifestyles' of the writers themselves. Only you can work these things out, with the help (as the acknowledgements pages of great numbers of books testify) of the people you live with.

Having said this, I hope I shall not be thought too inconsistent if I direct your attention to the historian E. H. Carr's excellent description of the way he works:

> Laymen – that is to say, non-academic friends or friends from other academic disciplines – sometimes ask me how the historian goes to work when he writes history. The commonest assumption appears to be that the historian divides his work into two sharply distinguishable phases or periods. First, he spends a long preliminary period reading his sources and filling his notebooks with facts: then, when this is over, he puts away his sources, takes out his notebooks and writes his books from beginning to end. This is to me an unconvincing and unplausible picture. For myself, as soon as I have got going on a few of what I take to be the capital sources, the itch becomes too strong and I begin to write – not necessarily the beginning, but somewhere, anywhere. Thereafter, reading and writing go on simultaneously. The writing is added to, subtracted from, reshaped, cancelled, as I go on reading. The reading is guided and directed and made fruitful by the writing: the more I write, the more I know what I am looking for, the better I understand the significance and relevance of what I find. Some historians probably do all this preliminary writing in their heads without using pen, paper or typewriter, just as some people play chess in their heads without recourse to board and chessmen: this is a talent which I envy, but cannot emulate. But I am convinced that, for any historian worth the name, the two processes of what economists call 'input' and 'output' go on simultaneously and are, in practice, parts of a single process.

It seems to me that the procedure Carr describes – reading a bit, writing when the itch comes, reading further and then rewriting – is worth taking seriously because it changes the nature of the problem from one concerned vaguely and generally with the act of writing to the more manageable one of writing *something*. The critical phase of the Carr cycle is getting the 'itch' to write, and for this there is indeed no generally applicable nettle. It is, I suppose, dependent in the first instance on becoming *interested* in what you are reading. And becoming interested in that, as we shall see in chapter 2, is partly dependent on how well you ask your questions and on that part of you that you bring to choosing the essay topic in the first place.

Think, then, of the times when something in a book has caught your attention sufficiently to make you insert an asterisk or underline the words. You may have been stimulated to make a marginal note or a note on a sheet of paper. This is the important moment. Here is the first faint itch. Instead of covering it over with salve and a book mark, begin to sharpen your ideas on it immediately. Even half a page which manages to deal in some way with the point and take in a few snatches of your other reading will suffice for a nucleus to be worked on later. Writing begets writing. As Goethe writes in the Prelude to *Faust*:

> Only engage, and then the mind grows heated –
> Begin it, and the work will be completed!

If you do this from time to time, your mind will be working constructively on the essay (even in periods off duty) and your attention will be shifted from the act to the matter when you come to write the essay as a whole. You will also have spread the load of facing that empty sheet of paper over many smaller, and more easily handled, instances.

There is, too, the role of discussion. Discussion is an essential part of academic work both as an informal preparation for writing and as writing's final justification. The coffee lounge and the seminar room, while quite distinct, are essential to the architecture of academe. But although the autocrats of the coffee table do not necessarily deserve a good hearing in the seminar room, they are at least preparing themselves for one asset of the business of writing – trying out and building up confidence in the phrases and arguments that will later be written down. If you feel you lack confidence you might be tempted to shirk these discussions in favour of solitary thinking. It is better not to. Informal discussion with friends and fellow students is an important preparation and a foil for the necessarily individual and solitary business of writing.

3 You and your subject matter

Whilst nearly everybody suffers to some degree from 'writer's block', we tend to vary in our ability to handle the four major elements of the writing process itself. We have seen that a good piece of academic writing needs to achieve a certain balance between these elements. So what you need to do in order to help you achieve this balance is to decide which of the elements you need to work at most. You might need to give most attention to establishing your own point of view on the topic and feeling able to hold to it with some degree of confidence. Or you might find manipulating your language to get it to say something sensible without too many chewed-up pencil ends and torn-up sheets of paper is the big problem. It could be that you find the main difficulty to be in structuring the essay in a coherent fashion out of the wads of notes you have taken, in being able to develop your ideas to 'fill up' the two or three thousand words required or, conversely, to cut down your four thousand words to the required length. And then you might be so worried about 'what they (the tutors) want' that you devote enormous amounts of energy to pleasing the reader and being unnecessarily meticulous in the conventional presentation of your work.

This list of common difficulties does not exhaust the possibilities. Furthermore, overcoming one of them might also require attention to one or two of the others. So, while the list does oversimplify somewhat, it is a good idea at this early stage to decide which of the writing problems apply most particularly to you. By identifying as well as you can your own strengths and weaknesses, you will be in a position to make the best use of this book.

We turn now to the problems of coming to terms with the subject matter in such a way that you will be able to develop confidence in establishing your own answer to the essay question.

The first, and perhaps most important, thing to bear in mind is that your tutor is not expecting in your essay the 'right' or the 'correct' answer to the question. It might be the case that there is a 'right' answer, but it is not likely that all of your tutors are going to be in complete agreement among themselves on what it is. Hence your job is not to find the right answer in the books, nor to find out what your tutor thinks is the right answer, but rather to use books and tutors to help you establish your best answer. This demands that you learn to exercise your faculty of judgement and to be as clear and explicit as you can about how you form your own judgements.

It is the manner in which we exercise this faculty of judgement that distinguishes academic enquiry at its best from much of the everyday writing we see around us and from much of the kind of writing your school teachers will probably have taught you. Much of your learning so far will have required you to produce accurate and coherent descriptions of things you have observed, things you have read and things you have been taught about. The questions, for the most part, have been raised by your teachers and your books. Now, these aspects of learning remain important in colleges and universities. But what may be new to you is the increasing responsibility thrust upon you to ask your own questions and to ANALYSE or DISCUSS (rather than just to describe) the objects of your enquiries and the statements that may be made about them. We begin to discover, for example, that what we had taken to be well-accepted facts about the world have an aura of uncertainty about them; they may turn out to be theories, interpretations or widely held beliefs rather than rock-solid 'facts'. We may discover, too, that facts about which there may be no serious debate can nevertheless have their importance valued or weighted differently by different authors or as a result of asking different questions. Such situations call for analysis and discussion, in which your own evaluations will become increasingly explicit, and in which descriptions, though present, play only a part. Two of the more common comments written by tutors on students' essays are 'Too descriptive' and 'Needs more analysis'.

Now, it is important to be quite clear about the nature of this process of judgement. It is not uncommon to see a student write 'In my opinion . . .', and a tutor write beside it 'We don't want your opinion.' Although this might seem to contradict what was said above about the importance of your own judgement, it does not. What the tutor is objecting to is 'opinion' unsupported by reason and evidence.

In chapter 2 we shall examine closely how, when you are first coming to grips with an essay topic, it is quite necessary to decide what your provisional opinion might be. Your opinion at this early stage of your work does not need to be justified at all. It can, as the philosopher Sir Karl Popper says, be no more than a 'prejudice'. You *must* bring your prejudices and opinions to bear on your provisional answer to the question. But, by the time your reading and your writing are finished, prejudice and opinion must have been converted into a reasoned judgement, which might be significantly different from your initial reaction to the essay topic. We can see how initial prejudice and opinion are transformed into judgement on a broad scale in this memoir by the Australian historian Manning Clark:

> I happened to have the good fortune to experience in
> childhood all the conflicts which were central to the human
> situation in Australia. My mother came from the old patrician,
> landed magnificoes in Australia; my father from the working
> class first of London, then of Sydney. So, years later when I
> read those words by Karl Marx, 'The history of all hitherto
> existing society is the history of class struggles', childhood
> memories made me say 'and that's true, too' just as years of

> reading and observation later were to fill in the details for that proposition about human society and raise doubts about what it leaves out.

Clark announces his prejudice in favour of Marx's dictum, a point of view governed by his own childhood experience and not by any academic method. That prejudice is absolutely necessary to Clark's history, but by itself it is not enough. It must be complemented by 'reading and observation' expressed in an objectively critical academic discourse which analyses the 'details' and comes to terms with the 'doubts'.

In beginning with our prejudices and opinions and then gradually converting them through reading and writing into considered judgements, we are committing a great deal of our own selves to the answer we give. We must be prepared to mean what we say. But we must also be able to feel a certain CONFIDENCE in our judgements. This confidence does not come so much from 'within' us as from the success with which our language formulates the judgement and backs it up. If you find it extremely difficult to get words onto the page, then what is probably at fault is your understanding of what you are trying to say or an insufficiently worked-out argument to support it. This can only be overcome by going back to your books or by forcing yourself to clarify your point of view by writing a short summary of it.

We have noticed above the need to take care that we mean what we say. But we must similarly take care, as the March Hare and the 'Mad' Hatter crossly pointed out to Alice, to say what we mean. There can be a yawning gulf between the two into which most of us can easily fall. When we have put our thoughts and judgements into words, we need to look at what is on the paper to find out whether what is there does indeed say what we meant to say.

Some academic writers rarely feel that they have got their language to say just what they intended, and a kind of secondary 'writer's block' sets in: the words are amended, scratched out, amended again and finally thrown into the waste paper basket – the whole process to be gone through again. If you spend inordinate amounts of time agonising over choices of word and sentence structure, it may well be that you are aiming for a kind of perfection and precision which is more than you can handle at the time. Perfection and precision for their own sakes are false goals in academic enquiry and writing (despite what some books say). You should cut and change only where you have decided that the meaning and structure of your argument is going to be significantly improved. A tendency to perfectionism, especially in relatively superficial aspects of writing, is often a sign of a lack of confidence. Confidence cannot be built up by presenting a perfectly grammatical exterior to your reader, but rather by trying out your ideas in the language that you can best muster on the occasion. If you feel that there is something wrong with that language, scrutinise first the idea you are trying to express.

If, on the other hand, you are the kind of writer who rarely changes anything and who, once the draft essay is completed, gladly forgets about it, you need to begin thinking very seriously about what writing an academic essay entails. Surveys of academic staff in Australian universities show that the average number of drafts they write of their own papers before submitting them to a journal for publication is between four and five. You do not have the time to do so many revisions; but you must make the time to do some. It is only when you read over your own work well after it has been composed that you will be able to see its shortcomings. This means that it is absolutely necessary to construct a timetable which provides that you finish the first draft of any essay well before it is due to be handed in. Some authorities recommend that you leave forty-eight hours between completing your first draft and going through it to prepare your second. This seems to me useful advice. Chapter 2 of this book is explicitly devoted to showing you how to approach your work so that you do not fall into the common pattern of finishing a first draft the night before the essay is due. Some people can produce excellence in a first draft; but they are probably the kinds of people referred to by E. H. Carr who can also play chess in their heads. If you do have difficulty in managing to say what you mean, you should pay particular attention to Part III of this book.

If you decide that clarifying the relationship between you, your subject matter and your language is a significant problem, then it would be a good idea to study closely what E. H. Carr says about how he approaches the writing of history (see p. 5). The essence of Carr's approach is that writing and reading (and, we might add, thinking) go on 'simultaneously' in a cycle. Writing begets reading and reading begets writing. The implication is that your knowledge and understanding are formulated *in* your language, not merely 'communicated' *by means of* language. In choosing our language we are choosing and establishing our point of view on the subject matter and our answer to the question raised by the essay topic. Each time you go round the cycle of reading, writing and thinking, you are gradually improving your understanding of the subject matter and your expression of that understanding in English. You are getting away from that Mephistophelian voice in you which says 'I understand this, but I just can't express it.' If you can't express it, the presumption must be that you don't sufficiently understand it.

4 You and your reader

While grappling with the problems of understanding and knowing the material, you have another matter to attend to. This is the interpersonal or communicative function of your writing. Writing is not *wholly* a problem in communication, as we have just seen; but now we must look at those aspects of writing which are governed by the need to present your ideas and your argument in a way that will help to 'get them across'. In some senses communicating successfully involves little more than learning and exploiting certain conventions of writing and presentation. In this respect the aim to be achieved is to write in such a way that the medium (paper, handwriting, spelling, setting-out, etc.) does not draw attention to itself. There is, however, one problem of communicating which will not go away quite so easily.

This problem is that of deciding whom you are writing for and whom you are writing to. The academic essay is in some respects an artificial task. Though you are ostensibly writing *to* a relatively depersonalised 'academic establishment', you are in effect writing *for* yourself. This is what assessment is about. The conflict thus engendered about the nature of your audience – department, tutor and self – makes the common injunction to writers, 'Know your audience', only a partly helpful truism. To make matters worse you are sometimes told to write as if a fellow student were going to read the essay, sometimes to write for the 'educated layman', and sometimes to write for academics in a different but related discipline. In desperation, or as a short cut, you may try to write *to* your tutor.

There are, however, certain dangers if you allow your tutor to dominate too much of your writing. Most of the dangers stem quite simply from the conventions of the teacher–student situation: writing in order to 'pass'. You may be tempted into plagiarising others' work if you believe the tutor will not recognise the source. While this approach may solve the immediate problem, it is no way to learn to write and may well catch up with you sooner or later. Or you may begin to ape the superficialities of the jargon of a discipline before you have really grasped the meaning of the language. By thus displaying a certain familiarity with this 'in-language', many believe the tutor will be taken in (which, of course, he or she can be). But this kind of travesty is often only too transparent. The third temptation in keeping tutors too much in mind is to toady to their theoretical predilections and opinions in the belief that this will earn you a higher grade. This last deserves more discussion.

It must first of all be acknowledged that, as any number of studies have shown, tutors can be quite unreliable in their assessments of written work. (Many departments recognise this and use various techniques for improving reliability.) Different tutors can vary significantly in the grade they allow to a given essay. This fact might encourage you to believe that the best way to get high grades is to flatter your tutor's opinions. It appears, however, that even an individual tutor may vary quite considerably in the value he or she attaches to the same piece of work from one time to another. It is also the case that some tutors are flattered by having you attack their own work, since in order to attack it you will need to have read it with care and attention. In my own experience the genuine conflicts about the substance of an opinion occur mostly over the work of graduate students. With undergraduates many such difficulties turn out to arise from misunderstandings not so much about the substance of a particular opinion as about its RELEVANCE to the essay question or about the quality of the student's analysis of supporting evidence. So before you assume a tutor is biased against you, do as much as you can to put into practice the concerns of this book, which seek to initiate you into the rites and conventions of academic debate.

But where there is considerable disparity between your own assessment of the value of your essay and the assessment the tutor makes, the best recourse is to argue it out with the tutor in question. Any good tutor should be prepared to give particular comments, to defend his or her judgement and to revise it if warranted. It is this matter of detailed comment that the student should insist on whether the examiner seems biased in favour or against. Marginal comment, a defence of the overall assessment, and some help with what you need to do to improve, is what you should seek first. Only then should you begin to worry about the tutor who does not like your opinions.

One matter on which you should always submit to the wishes of your tutor concerns the conventions of presentation: the preferred FORMS of footnoting and referencing, and of headings, margins and type of paper, the quality of your proofreading and spelling, the clarity of your handwriting or the accuracy of your typing, and so on. (If your handwriting is better than your typing, it is usually better to write your essays by hand until your typing skills improve.) Good communication is obtained in part by reducing to a minimum what engineers call 'noise' in the channel – anything that will distract the reader from the object of concentration. It is customary for manuals of composition to justify these matters in terms of courtesy to the reader. But there is also a simple psychological factor. If your reader's attention is constantly distracted by undecipherable handwriting, spelling mistakes or poor referencing, there will be less processing capacity in his or her brain to devote to the substance of your essay. Like so many of the things we discuss in connection with writing, successful communication is a matter of achieving an optimal balance in a given situation. It is even possible to make your presentation too perfect. If your cultural background has placed great emphasis on courtesy and convention, it is quite possible that you will expend a disproportionate amount of effort on parading immaculately labelled headings, brightly polished typing and crisply pressed footnotes. The excellence of the presentation may make it rather too clear that you have neglected more important aspects of your writing.

5 Your language: form and structure

So far, we have seen how aspects of language enter into such problems as how you establish your point of view on a topic, how you come to understand and express your subject matter, and how you establish a 'line of communication' with your reader. Now we look at some problems of writing which arise out of the nature of language itself. To make language work for you, it is a good idea to learn something of its forms and structures, just as cabinet-makers need to understand the properties of their timbers. The forms we are concerned with operate on two levels – that of the sentence and that of larger units of discourse like the paragraph and the essay as a whole. There are ways in which we use words, grammar and discourse to organise our diverse ideas into a coherent unity. Every piece of academic writing should strive for this unity.

A well-organised piece of writing reveals that the writer has established a pattern of relationships between the individual parts and between the parts and the whole composition. When we read, we are often dimly aware that the author of our book has achieved this formal balance without our being able to say exactly how. When we write we are often uncomfortably aware that we haven't achieved it. Sometimes we begin to realise that our thinking and writing are just 'going round in circles'. We start to repeat ourselves unnecessarily, contradict ourselves, or fail to show the connections between ideas. We become aware that, whenever we arrive at the end of a section of the essay, or of a paragraph or even of a sentence, we do not know where to turn next or how to establish a connection between what is written and what is to be written. We become more and more unable to decide between what should be included in the essay and what should be left out. Paragraphs become very, very long or very, very short. Sentences become long and convoluted, such that the end has quite forgotten the beginning. More or less random mistakes in spelling, punctuation and some aspects of grammar begin to creep in. Overall, we get that feeling that our writing does not 'flow', that some aspect of its structure has collapsed.

The first difficulty we face is in learning to recognise when these symptoms are present. Sometimes they are not particularly apparent to us while we are writing, only revealing themselves when we read the piece over later. Sometimes our own sense of form is not sufficiently developed to enable us to see aspects of our problem at all. We learn these things by having our writing criticised by others, and by absorbing gradually from our reading a sense of what good writing 'feels' like. It is therefore often only a vague sense of discomfort, in the first instance, that alerts us to the situation in our own writing.

When this discomfort is felt, we may be able to go back over our work and describe in some detail what is going wrong – perhaps by identifying such particular symptoms as are listed above. For example, an almost invariable sign that something is wrong is a series of either very long or very short paragraphs – and this condition is easy to spot. But being able to locate and identify the symptom is often not enough, since local tinkering with, say, paragraph boundaries (running short ones together or chopping long ones into parts) does not always get at the heart of the problem. This is the point at which we often have to decide to cross out the whole passage and start again.

Far from seeking to improve the form for its own sake, our rewriting gives us a chance to improve our understanding of the SUBJECT we are writing about. There are aesthetes who fiddle with the form of their work to gain purely formal satisfactions, and there should indeed be something of the aesthete in all writers. But the chance to rewrite is the chance to conceive afresh what it is we are trying to say. And that means searching for an idea which becomes the new focus of attention, a new unifying vision of the subject, around which the parts which once seemed so intractable will now cluster more or less easily. In short, to heed the formal signals of distress gives us the opportunity to think of a better answer to the question. The satisfactions of this are great.

Nobody, however, will deny the desire to get things more or less right the first time. If good structure depends, as we have seen, so critically on finding that elusive unifying idea, good structure therefore has its origins in your very first confrontation with the essay topic. There are, of course, many questions which can only be faced and resolved as the occasion arises. But that central issue of the overall organisation of your essay and its major parts is not something that can be added in as you 'write up' a draft. If you do recognise in yourself the 'scissors-and-paste' syndrome and the other symptoms of poor structure in your essay-writing, you may well need to pay especial attention to the way in which you come to terms with the essay topic.

Form and structure enter into most aspects of writing. Even so, this book, it should be clear, is about much more than getting the right words and grammatical forms into the right places. To write well you will also need progressively to learn about yourself and the way your own mind works, about the ways in which you attain to knowledge, and about the academic culture in which you and your readers live. Dealing adequately with all these claims to the attention demands that you gradually work out for yourself a set of procedures and conditions that will not only improve your efficiency but also open up new, more interesting and more subtle ways of approaching your work. You will find in this book various hints and recommendations about what you might take account of in trying to reach that happy state where you can even enjoy the taxing process of writing. The particular synthesis you make of the issues treated here is, however, your own responsibility. The success with which all these matters are resolved will be apparent in the artefact that emerges: every piece of your writing you preserve will always remain an articulate testimony to your state of mind when you wrote it. This is what makes writing – even if 'only' another academic essay – an attempt to deal not only with a 'topic' but with knowledge itself, with other people and with yourself.

Part I

*Reflection
and
Research*

2
Reflection: asking questions and proposing answers

I have always preferred to reflect
upon a problem before reading on it.
JEAN PIAGET

1 Speculative thinking and writing

This is a chapter about thinking and reflection. It comes first in our consideration of essay-writing technique because it is the first of the many activities in writing an essay that you should engage in. Many, if not most, students leave the really hard thinking until after they have done the reading or research. They do this in the belief that one can't think constructively until all the information is gathered and the writing of the final draft is due to begin. This is not so, as the quotation above from the philosopher and psychologist Jean Piaget suggests.

One of the most important abilities needed to master essay-writing in the humanities and social sciences is the ability to ASK QUESTIONS of the essay topic itself as well as of the books you will read. If you can develop a facility in asking questions and in reflecting on likely answers to those questions, it is possible for a general shape for your essay (though not its precise content) to become evident to you even before you have begun on any detailed reading. The procedure is something like this:

1 Choose an essay topic because it interests you. Such a topic is more likely to be one about which you might already have a few questions or ideas.
2 Ask questions of the topic: try to work out what it is driving at, what is meant by various words or phrases in it, and what kinds

of connection there may be between the various issues it raises. Do no more reading (or better, 'consulting' of a few very basic source books) than is necessary to suggest possible answers to your questions.

3 Propose to yourself a few likely answers to the question raised by the topic and write them down in no more than a sentence or two. Then choose which seems to be the best. Discussing the topic with friends is very useful at this stage.

4 Develop this answer into a short paragraph which, so far as you can, lists the reasons for choosing the answer you did or some of the facts and ideas that you think might support it.

5 Regard this paragraph as no more than a hypothesis about, a proposal for, or a forecast of, your eventual answer. It might well lay the foundations of the opening paragraph of your essay, but it will need to be tested out (and probably changed) by your detailed reading – which should not begin until now.

The aim of this chapter is to show you how to do these things. You need to be aware at the outset that you may not find it easy to master and apply these techniques of reflective questioning and exploratory writing. You may well be strongly tempted to scurry back to the apparent security of your books and the deceptive sense of being 'busy' in the library, leaving the hard thinking until a night or two before the essay is due. There are two main reasons why you should resist this temptation.

The first is that hard preliminary thinking and writing leads eventually to better essays. The second is that it makes you more efficient in your work, and consequently saves you important time.

It might seem that a procedure which asks you to produce a draft paragraph which almost certainly will have to be changed, and perhaps wholly scrapped, is academically worthless, not to say inefficient. This is not so. You will remember we saw in chapter 1 that writing and thinking beget more writing and thinking. Now if your thinking is not constrained by the need to write down what comes of it, it will usually be fairly undisciplined, not to say idle and disjointed. Writing is your best way of discovering whether you have actually captured a thought and whether it is any good. Improvement does not emerge from nothing, but by changing what exists. The single chief value of a speculative answer in a short paragraph is not just that it might become the foundation of the eventual answer but that it gives you something to change, something to improve on by further reading, thinking and writing. This is what leads to better essays.

Having a speculative answer leads to a more efficient use of time in a number of ways. Your reading becomes quicker and you don't lose concentration on a book so easily. Since you have a better idea of what is likely to be relevant, you spend less time taking mountains of notes that eventually turn out to be quite useless. Thirdly, you do not spend valuable hours towards the end of the research period hunting desperately through the library in the vain Micawber-like hope that 'something will turn up' to show you how to write your answer. Finally, there is long-standing psychological evidence that once you have consciously articulated certain issues to be worked on, your subconscious mind will beaver away at them whilst you are doing other things, with the result that every now and again an answer or an improvement will pop to the surface. (The philosopher Bertrand Russell prepared himself for these happy occasions by carrying round a little notebook in which to write these ideas down, pages from which he would later insert in an appropriate file.) In this way you save time because your subconscious can be working on one essay while your conscious attention is engaged on another.

The steps summarised above we shall now treat in more detail.

2 Choosing a topic

Your choice of a topic on which to write should be governed most importantly by your own personal interest and 'prejudice'. Your only guide in this matter is yourself. Some people think that if you are too committed to a subject you will write an essay which is too strongly influenced by your desire to entrench a particular point of view, irrespective of evidence. This should not worry you, provided that you draw an important distinction. This is a distinction between your interest in the subject as being worthy of study and a commitment to be as detached as you can when you eventually come to analyse the evidence which supports one or another answer to the question. The early stages of preparing an essay dealt with in this chapter are purely private. So choosing a topic, like your first reflections on it, can be governed by as much self-interest and prejudice as you care to allow. It would be much more a problem if you find that none of the topics on a list interests you. If that happens, you should try to work one out for yourself on some aspect of the course that does interest you and then gain your tutor's approval of it.

There are some subsidiary issues which might enter into your choice of topic, and which might influence you in favouring one over others of equal interest. The first of these issues are somewhat negative ones.

One consideration that might weigh heavily with you is the relevance of a topic to the syllabus as a whole and to end-of-course examinations in particular. The 'pragmatic' student might decide that to write on such a topic effectively kills two birds with one stone, a decision which justifies the argument 'What am I studying for if not to get my degree or diploma in the most efficient way possible?' There is nothing wrong with this argument provided that it is not allowed to override the importance of being interested in the subject itself. Some recent research into student performance in universities suggests that to be too 'syllabus-bound' eventually works against academic success. If you pursue your interests within the broad scope of the courses you are taking, you will ultimately perform better than if you keep your gaze too firmly fixed on the qualification at the end of it all. Bear it in mind that enthusiasm for a subject will be manifest in your writing, and will convey itself to a grateful reader.

For similar reasons you should not reject an interesting topic because it has not yet been covered in class. Nor, having chosen such a topic, should you postpone the beginning of your work until it is. Lecturers and tutors rarely address their comments to the precise question or questions raised by an essay topic. This is not necessarily neglect – and may be quite deliberate, since they do not wish to read many essays which uniformly echo the lectures. Hence nothing that they say is likely to be of any more initial benefit to you than what is contained in an introductory book on the subject. Even if the classes do address issues of direct relevance to a topic, you must realise that the lecturer is not giving you *the* answer to the question but his or her answer, which must be analysed in exactly the same way as you will analyse other answers in your written sources. Indeed, if you have done plenty of preliminary work before the classes take the matter up, you will be in a much better position to assess the value, the relevance and the significance of what is said.

All this having been said, there are certain other practical considerations to be taken into account. Other things being equal, in courses with many students unpopular topics may be worth a closer look. This is because competition for the available references in the library will be less fierce and because the essays written on them will bear a relative freshness to the reader. Another rule of thumb is that, for some students, topics worded in a very general way are often harder to write on well than topics in which the issues are set out more precisely. General or broad topics leave to you so much more of the questioning process itself and the evaluation of the best questions to ask. The more clearly the questions are focused, the easier it is to control the RELEVANCE of the answers. Against this, it must be said, topics which are very precise in their demands may not allow quite so much scope for you to develop your own point of view. The price of safety may be a certain constriction of freedom.

If you are asked not to choose a topic from a prepared list but to devise one for yourself, you face, at bottom, much the same problems as those we have already discussed. They may, however, be considerably magnified; it is really much harder to ask good questions than it is to answer them. Your interest in the subject is still paramount. Even so, it has to be weighed against such practical and intellectual matters as the availability of sufficient evidence or data relative to the broadness of the topic, the extent to which it allows theoretical or methodological questions of interest to the discipline to be asked of it, the amount of time available and the projected length of the paper. Factors such as these need to be nicely balanced, so you must discuss them in some detail with your tutor before you finally settle on the wording of your topic. Nor should you be afraid to seek a change in the wording of the topic if your early investigations lead you into major problems.

3 Kinds of question

An object, event, situation, concept or idea becomes an object of ENQUIRY because someone has raised an interesting or significant question about it. The object does not have to be a 'new discovery'. It might have lain around for years or centuries as a 'fact' or as part of our accustomed intellectual furniture until the thought strikes a fresh mind that there is about it an unresolved question with interesting implications. Indeed, far from having to wait until a novel object is brought in for study – like a piece of moon rock from an Apollo mission – it is by raising new questions about existing objects of knowledge that we often uncover new objects whose existence was unknown.

Academic enquiry, as we have seen, proceeds in the first instance by asking questions. Your essay topics are examples of these questions. Just as your tutors ask questions of you by the essay topics they set, so you must learn to ask questions both of the essay topic itself and of the various books you use in your reading for the essay. It is the answers to these questions which, when integrated in a coherent fashion, become an essay. Skill in asking good questions (a 'good' question is one which opens up a fruitful line of enquiry) is something that comes with practice, knowledge and experience in the disciplines you are studying. There is no method or formula for coming up with really good questions. It is possible, nevertheless, that by learning to ring the changes on the question words we use, various lines of thought will be opened up and – an important consideration for many of us – this will help overcome 'writer's block'. These question words are 'what', 'which', 'who', 'whom', 'where', 'when', 'how', 'why', 'to what extent' and 'how far'.

What

'What' has a number of functions. Typically it asks for clarification about some phenomenon that is being REFERRED to, for example 'What is expressionism?' This is a request to establish the connection between a name (a word) and an object or phenomenon 'in the world' which has been observed: we say the *name* refers to the *object*, as the names 'morning star' or 'Venus' refer to a particular point of light in the sky. Some 'what' requests may seek a DESCRIPTION of a *particular* object or idea in answer to them:

> What was the character of the social philosophy which shaped the Poor Law Amendment Act of 1834?

> What is Rawls's theory of justice?

Other 'what' questions look for more *generalised* or *universal* DEFINITIONS and THEORIES:

> What is justice? (this is the question Rawls asked)

> What is a dialect and what is a language? Can any universally applicable criteria be used to distinguish them?

Definitions are treated at length in chapter 9.

Who, whom

These two words are also requests for an IDENTIFICATION, this time, of course, only of people or groups of people. 'Who' queries the identity of people who do things or who are the responsible AGENTS for some event. 'Whom', by contrast, raises a question about the people AFFECTED by an action or event, sometimes called the 'affected' or the 'patients'. A question about the one will very often raise a question about the other. Notice, too, that the range of a 'whom' question can be considerably widened by prefacing it with a preposition (e.g. to, for, by, with, amongst):

> Who was ultimately responsible for the deportation of Jews in Lyons to Auschwitz?

> To whom did Clement Attlee's policy particularly appeal during the British election campaign of 1945?

Where, when

'Where' and 'when' query aspects of the LOCATION, TIME and DURATION of objects and events. Like 'who' and 'whom', these questions do not commonly turn up in the essay topics undergraduate students are asked to write on. Nevertheless, they are invaluable questions to turn upon the topics you are set, since your answer may well depend critically on whether certain conditions of place, time and duration can be satisfied. If asked, for example, to assess whether the 'pacification' programme in the Vietnam War was a success, you might answer that it was, but only for a certain period and in certain parts of the country. Being able to specify times and places reliably may be just as important in answering some academic questions as it is in a criminal trial. Asking questions about 'where' and 'when' can also raise detailed issues of distribution, extent, frequency, regularity and other important topics in a variety of disciplines.

How

'How' can be interpreted in a number of ways. First it can be a request for a DESCRIPTION of a PROCESS (rather than of an object or phenomenon):

How did General Douglas MacArthur honour his promise to return to the Philippines?

How does Shakespeare achieve the integration of plot and subplot in *King Lear*?

A second sense of 'how' can be paraphrased as 'in what respects'. This is more like the kind of description we considered when discussing 'what' – a request for various characteristics or features:

How has the decipherment of Linear B tablets improved our understanding of the Mycenaean religion?

How does the structure of society contribute to adolescent delinquency?

Finally 'how' may demand an EXPLANATION, and this sense of 'how' is often hardly distinguishable from 'why'. Physical scientists commonly say they make no distinction between 'how' and 'why' questions, or if they do, they limit themselves to 'how' questions, the answers to which are to be sought in the mechanisms of nature rather than human will, intention or motives. Humanities and social science students will therefore meet this sense of 'how' in those disciplines whose subject matter and methods of enquiry more closely approach those of natural science:

How does the 'chunking' of information help to explain individual differences in short-term memory performance?

How were the Himalayan mountains formed?

How are certain aspects of social structure affected by the physical environment in which a society lives?

In the examples above it is possible to detect a shifting about in the meaning of 'how', even though each could be rewritten as a 'why' question. In the first, 'how' could simply be replaced by 'why'. In the second, 'how' might initially appear to require merely a description of processes. But the answer to this question would need to examine why the Himalayas are formed as they are or, alternatively, what caused them to be formed as they are. The third illustrates another sense in which 'how' can be interpreted as 'why'. This question can be paraphrased 'Why do certain aspects of social structure reflect the physical environment in which a society lives?' An answer to this question would need to examine the underlying RELATIONS between social structure and the environment rather than anything that could properly be called a cause. (For another example of such an explanation see (4) under the list of explanation types below.) All these uses of 'how' seek varying kinds of explanation.

Why

If the meaning of 'how' has seemed to be rather complex, that of 'why' is much more so. 'Why' is a request for an EXPLANATION, and, very often, a THEORY. One of the difficulties with explanations, however, is that there are quite a few different kinds. That is to say, there are various quite different ways of answering a 'why' question, depending on the disciplines that you are studying, and even on schools of thought within disciplines. An explanation in anthropology can be a very different thing from an explanation in history. And an approach to explanation which is acceptable to the department of anthropology in one university or college might be discouraged in the anthropology department of another. Some of the commoner types of explanation are the following.

1. Causal explanations – what were the causes of some event or phenomenon? For example, 'Why did a militant movement advocating votes for women emerge in England during the Edwardian era?'

2. Purposive explanations – what were the reasons, aims, purposes or intentions of those responsible for some action, event, phenomenon, etc? For example, 'Why have social anthropologists traditionally paid so much attention to the study of kinship?'

3 Functional explanations – what function does something have, or what role does it play, within a larger system of which it is a part? For example, 'Why does the tone of voice change so often and so dramatically in T. S. Eliot's *The Waste Land*?'

4 Structural explanations – what abstract and universal rules, codes or laws account for the relations between features of a system and which of these rules generate its structure? For example, 'Why is the industrial wealth of the First World inseparable from the rural poverty of the Third World?'

5 Deductive explanations – what combinations of conditions or premises allow us to infer a logical conclusion? For example, 'Why are utilitarians committed to opposing capital punishment?'

To what extent, how much, how far, how significant

There are many ways of asking questions that call for a JUDGE-MENT, ASSESSMENT or EVALUATION. These are some of them. The simplest idea of evaluating is to rank a phenomenon on a scale – say, cold to hot, useless to useful, bad to good – which gives some measure of degree. Those questions that begin 'How . . .' will give you the criterion or scale on which the phenomenon has to be assessed, for example quantity in the case of 'how much', temperature in the case of 'how hot', significance in the case of 'how significant', and so on. 'To what extent' and 'how far' are questions that leave to you the task of deciding the best criteria by which to evaluate the issue in question:

'. . . Mill's open-mindedness was too large for the system he inherited' (A. D. Lindsay). To what extent did John Stuart Mill differ from early utilitarian attitudes to state intervention in social and economic affairs?

To what extent do you believe the Australian mass media play a key role in social control?

How far is the rise in suicide rates during times of economic prosperity attributable to people's earlier experiences during economic recession?

Reflection: asking questions and proposing answers

> How important is the Porter to the main plot of Shakespeare's *Macbeth*? Is he just comic 'relief'?

In the first and last of these topics you are given a hint about the criterion to be examined – qualities of open-mindedness and comic 'relief'. But when you ask evaluative questions yourself, the most appropriate criteria must be supplied by you.

Which

'Which' is used to do two related things – to IDENTIFY and to compel one to DECIDE. Identifying is the counterpart of referring. Whereas with 'what' questions we have a name and we wish to know the object, identifying involves fitting a name to the object or description before us:

> Which of the attitudes to capital punishment is favoured by utilitarians?

Simple identification itself involves little more than pointing to the desired object in a line-up. Interesting 'which' questions are raised when it is not easy to make a decision:

> Which of the two common theories that attempt to account for the origins of cities is the more plausible?

Such a question asks one to COMPARE and CONTRAST the two theories and make a *choice* between them. Choosing requires one to establish appropriate criteria according to which the final decision is made: if I have to decide whether today is colder than yesterday I look to the thermometer readings, which give me a measure according to the criterion of temperature, and perhaps also to other measurements which are criteria – such as the wind chill factor and humidity. DECIDING is therefore an EVALUATIVE activity, too, in which one is explicitly required to COMPARE and CONTRAST the criteria on which the evaluation is to be made. The criterion to be used in answering the question above is plausibility. The next problem is to work out how plausibility can be defined for the purpose of this essay.

This completes our sketch of the typical question words. It is important to keep in mind the fact that just as these sorts of question (except for 'who', 'whom', 'where' and 'when') commonly appear in essay topics set by the tutor, they must, in turn, be used by you on the essay topic itself. Hence, in the topic on the origin of cities given above, the first question that needs to be asked of it is a 'what' question: 'What are these "two common theories"?'

An essay topic phrased not as a question but as a statement (or quotation) followed by an instruction to discuss, examine, analyse, comment on, consider, account for, assess, etc. is really no different. (The differences in meaning between these instructions are not especially significant – so do not take too seriously those books on study skills which try to make fine distinctions between them.) Such instructions are open invitations to the writer to formulate from the statement or quotation the most fruitful question to ask. Hence it is best to treat them as questions.

Some topics allow you considerable latitude to formulate your own question. For example, the widespread exercise in English literature in which the student is given a poem and asked to comment on it (do a 'practical criticism') is as much a test of your ability to ask fruitful and appropriate questions as it is to write answers to them: 'What does this poem really mean?' 'Is it a satire or is it only pretending to be?' 'Why does so much of the imagery seem to be pulling in a different direction from the "argument"?' 'How is the conflict that seems to be going on resolved, and is this resolution successful?' 'Is this poem a sentimental platitude?' Having formulated the most interesting question about the poem by which to guide the essay, you can then ask lots of others which might help with the discussion and contribute to the answer.

We are now going to examine the procedures you might adopt in the systematic unpacking of an essay topic and the proposing of an answer. Remember that the immediate purpose of this kind of reflection is not to write an essay but to do as much as possible to *prepare* for the writing of an essay. Your aim is to allow a free play of your mind on the topic, trying to forecast as well as you can the general line an essay might take.

The premium at this stage of your work is to be put on thinking, on the analysis of likely possibilities, on 'bold conjectures', and on the knowledge, experience and motherwit you already possess. Only when some of these things have clearly failed should you yield to the temptation to open a book, and even then it should be a general book in which you search for just that information you need to get your thinking to bite. Thinking is, as we saw earlier in this chapter, a difficult thing to do, particularly if you find formal reasoning in something of a vacuum not your natural style. It can, however, be practised. Bear it in mind that your essay will be *your* 'best' answer, not an answer to be found pat in some book. Therefore, you might as well begin with yourself in confrontation with your chosen topic.

4 Coming to terms with an essay topic

4.1 *Making up your mind*

Your essay will be your *answer* to a question – not a general consideration of issues and facts that might pertain to some aspects of the topic. Answering a question means that you must be prepared to make a decision – no matter which question words are used. And any decision runs the risk of embarrassing the person who made it. You might show considerable care, discretion and caution about how far out on a limb you are prepared to go, but climb out on the limb you must. The earlier you try it out, the less painful and embarrassing it is to have it snap under you. The path to learning is littered with the bruised bodies of crestfallen scholars. Nobody but the scholar with the bruises and fallen crest takes much notice of that; but you owe it to yourself to make as many as you can of the mistakes from which you learn *before* you present your final draft for assessment. An 'essay', in one of its early meanings, is a trial.

With one kind of question, for example 'Did the White Australia policy become whiter between 1901 and 1921?', one has no option but to choose either 'yes' or 'no'. The answer can be hedged about with all sorts of qualifications, and that is expected. But to respond 'Maybe it did and maybe it didn't' is not to answer at all. The best thing to do is to try out an answer and see whether it holds up.

The same principle applies to any question, irrespective of whether it is framed in yes/no terms. The fact that many essay topics do not enforce such a clearcut decision should not delude you:

> Human nature may be the foundation of politics, but the state is the key unit of political organisation. Discuss the role of the state.

Here you are challenged to agree or disagree with the proposition contained in the first sentence. You might agree that it is necessary to separate 'foundation of politics' and 'unit of political organisation' and that the latter is more important. Or you might not: you might argue that the state can never be much more than the sum of the individual human natures that make it up. Such a decision has to be made.

Even the most innocent of questions that appear to ask for no more than a straightforward description can contain the seeds of a controversy on which you will have to make up your mind:

> How did General Douglas MacArthur honour his promise to return to the Philippines?

With a little bit of reflection you can propose a workmanlike description of the likely processes: MacArthur's strategic and tactical decisions; battles won and lost with politicians, other generals and the enemy; his method of working; his character; his effectiveness as a field commander; and so on. But the very fact that this list can grow so easily should warn you that some of these things deserve more EMPHASIS than others. That is to say, you must *decide* provisionally which of these factors – or which combination of them – *best* explain MacArthur's success, and which are less important.

One of the popular images of an academic or a scholar is that when you ask him a question you can never get a straight answer. He responds with an 'on the one hand' and an 'on the other'. This is a caricature with a certain element of truth. As one burrows more deeply into a question it becomes harder and harder to answer a question simply and confidently. When England was wracked by the claims and counterclaims of Catholic and Protestant dogma during the early seventeenth century, it was said of one scholar, William Chillingworth, that he 'contracted such a habit of doubting that by degrees he grew confident of nothing'. While allowing that the answers to many questions may be very complicated, you must nevertheless resist succumbing to this state of mind.

4.2 Problems of meaning and knowledge

Most people find that, while it is easy enough to propose an immediate tentative answer to some questions, others raise knotty problems of meaning and interpretation that need to be dealt with first. This will happen particularly where the topic makes use of terms with which you are not familiar, where it is worded in a vague or ambiguous manner, and where you feel you have so little background knowledge of the issues it raises that to speculate about a likely answer is impossible. We shall treat each of these situations in turn.

Clarifying the meaning of terms

When you are considering the meanings of terms in your essay topics, a major decision you have to make is whether any of them have a special meaning or use in the discipline you are studying. This applies equally to what look like ordinary everyday words as it does to those recherché terms (e.g. recherché, moiety, phoneme, hermeneutic, existential) that are rarely to be found in everyday language. Indeed, it is the more common words that pose a problem, simply because their special uses are more likely to be overlooked. 'Class', 'language', 'democracy', 'comedy', 'the market', 'structure', 'function', 'justice' are examples of terms whose uses can vary considerably in different disciplines. Moreover, they are examples of terms for which there are no generally accepted or conclusive definitions.

From this distinction between terms that are of no particular significance to a given discipline and terms that are, there follows an important lesson to learn. If you do not know the meaning of a word in your essay topic, look it up first in an ordinary desk dictionary. If you have no reason to believe it is of special significance to the discipline, you need not pursue the matter any further. (In particular, you should never bother to define such words in the essay, since your reader does not want to know the common definition of an unproblematic word.) You have merely used the dictionary to help you interpret the meaning of the essay topic. If, on the other hand, you suspect the word does have some special significance, you must go to your textbooks or to specialised dictionaries to find out what the problems with defining the term might be; your interpretation of the meaning of the essay topic as a whole might depend critically on which definition or interpretation of the term you use.

We have seen already (p. 27) how some essay topics will almost solely demand discussion of the meaning of a term or set of terms:

> What is the difference between literary language and everyday language? Illustrate your discussion by close reference to a few selected texts.

Your questioning of the meaning of the two significant terms in this topic ('literary' and 'everyday') is pretty well the questioning of the meaning of the topic as a whole. In other topics some formidable problems of definition need to be approached *in the course of* dealing with other issues raised in the question:

> 'In Western countries the upper class is no longer a ruling class.' Discuss.

What is 'class'? What grounds are there for distinguishing 'upper class' from 'ruling class'? How does the distinction fit into any of the widely canvassed theories of class? Only by dealing with questions such as these can one say very much of significance about Western society: whether there ever was an 'upper class' in all Western countries, how it ruled, and whether and in what respects it has been replaced by a 'ruling class' which is significantly different. The limitations of dictionaries – even specialised ones – will be obvious in dealing with issues like these.

There are few less inspiring beginnings to an essay than 'Let us first define our terms', particularly if that definition is taken from a standard dictionary. If there is a major problem of definition or interpretation, it will have to be DISCUSSED, letting the issues emerge during the course of the discussion. More is said about this matter in chapter 4 (p. 95) and chapter 9.

The meaning of an essay topic as a whole

The meaning of an essay topic is not to be discovered simply by adding up, as it were, the meanings of the individual words that compose it. As we have noticed before, the important requirement is that you try to understand the tutor's intent behind the topic. You should learn to ask yourself 'What is the author of this topic driving at in asking this question?' (Remember that essay topics are not drawn from some sort of Bible, but are formulated by your teachers because they probably think that in them lies an interesting or debatable issue on which they want to read your judgement. They reflect your teachers' changing interests in what they think worthwhile questions to ask, and so the topics of today are often quite different from those of yesterday.) While it is useful and important to underline what appear to be the significant words in a topic, this by itself is not enough. The topic on the nature of the state, mentioned earlier, is a good enough example:

> Human nature may be the foundation of politics, but the state
> is the key unit of political organisation. Discuss the role of the
> state.

Here it is necessary to recognise the force of the word 'but' in
assessing what the topic is driving at. The author of the proposition in the topic is suggesting that the problems of human
nature, though fundamental to politics, can safely be set aside if
we are to find out what 'political organisation' really is. Hence
you have to work out for yourself whether the proposed contrast
(signalled by the 'but') between 'politics' and 'political organisation' is one that you are prepared to defend. This leads, as we
saw, to deciding whether politics is the sum of the individual
human natures that make up the state, or whether there is an
organisational dimension which transcends the demands of
human nature. Reduced to its bare bones, you might interpret
the question as asking whether you are a traditional liberal/
conservative exponent of individualist views or whether you
think the needs of the state must override those of the individuals in it. All this rather deep philosophising hinges on your
understanding the force of 'but' and the contrast it marks
between politics and political organisation. So it is just as
important to underline the 'but' as it is to underline the more
substantive terms.

You need also to look for the ambiguities in essay topics.
Sometimes these are accidental (do not assume that every essay
topic you see is well worded). But often they test your ability to
pick up the ambiguity and to find the real issue beneath it. Here
is an example:

> Why was George III accused of attempting to subvert the
> constitution?

The ambiguity here hinges on the question word 'Why'. There
are two questions here, neither of which – it is important to
realise – is 'Why did George III attempt to subvert the constitution?' It would be possible to choose one or the other or,

perhaps more interestingly, to tackle both. On the one hand, the question could read 'What were his accusers' reasons for saying he had tried to subvert the constitution?' On the other, it could be 'What (if anything) did George III actually do to try to subvert the constitution?' The first looks the more fruitful interpretation; but by combining both we shall be able to examine the gap that opens between any attempt George III might have made to subvert the constitution and the strength of his accusers' denunciations of him. The use of the passive voice ('was accused') creates an indeterminacy. *Who* accused him? Was it only contemporaries with their own political motives, or has this chorus been joined by subsequent politicians and historians? You will notice that the way in which I have expressed my interpretation of the question is already leading me towards a defence of George III against his critics.

If, after plenty of the kind of consideration of the topic we are discussing in this chapter, you cannot decide between a few reasonable interpretations, you should consult your tutor. Do not forget, nevertheless, that such a consultation is not a substitute for saying in the essay itself *how* you have chosen to interpret the topic and, if you can, *why* this seems the more fruitful interpretation (see chapter 4).

Background knowledge

Since each of us brings a partly idiosyncratic general knowledge and experience to a given topic, it is not possible to generalise about the point at which any one of us should open a book. But, in putting off any reading until we have worked out a few *particular* things we want to find out about, we can create mental space for the kind of *formal* analysis of the topic we shall study in the next section. Postponing detailed reading also gives us the chance to articulate whatever general knowledge and experience we are able to bring to the issue in question. The list of suggestions I put forward on p. 35 to account for how General MacArthur honoured his promise to return to the Philippines owes nothing to reading I have done on MacArthur. I have never read any book on MacArthur. But I have read books on, and memoirs by, other generals from Cromwell to Eisenhower. I have seen (as most of us have) many TV movies about modern war, and read newspaper articles. It is in such very general storehouses of the mind that we can look for a few tentative ideas to get our thinking going. The richer and more articulate your initial 'personal response', the better your library research will be.

When we think of knowledge we do not only have in mind a store of information about a subject, though that is clearly part of it. Knowledge also includes knowing how to APPROACH information. All disciplines develop particular approaches to their material, and these approaches constitute part of the definition of a discipline. If you look back at the list of issues raised about MacArthur, you will see that it is made up of a number of approaches to, or CATEGORIES of, the study of military general*ship*. There may be others (to be found in one's detailed reading), but that list is enough to get us going.

A source of very broad categories that can help you organise your initial thoughts is the table of contents in a general introductory text or a book for 'preliminary reading'. So we find, for example, that social anthropology of the 'British school' tends to approach the study of society using such categories as kinship, family organisation and marriage, government and law, the production and exchange of food and goods (economics), religion and magic, and the effect of the physical environment. A short introduction to the study of literature recommended to first-year students in my own university lists in its table of contents diction, figurative language, narrative point of view, irony, tone, pattern, and some examples of genre – epic and mock heroic. I can think of other things that this list could have included, so it is a good idea to COMPARE such books. Finer categories of analysis will be found in the body of the book itself (e.g. the differing points of view a novelist might adopt in his narrative), and these you will need to seize on as you develop your ideas for the essay. These categories are not necessarily a template that can be slapped down to cut out an essay on any topic.

The mere listing of categories may ignore the complexity of the relations between them. For example, in some societies the exchange of certain goods in certain patterns has social, political and religious (or ritual) significance as well as an economic function; the diction, tone and the implied speaker's 'voice' interact in very different and complex ways in individual poems. Hence an essay simply organised under these categories may distort the subject or miss the dynamics of its unity. Even so, they are a necessary part of the process by which you can get a purchase on the subject matter of the essay.

4.3 Formal meaning: the logical shape of possible answers

We shall now study the ways in which categories or classes of things can enter into various formal *relations* of meaning. There is much to be said for analysing essay topics formally since this kind of analysis can often throw up for consideration alternative answers which we might not otherwise think of.

By 'formal meaning' here we are thinking particularly of the meanings of a few logical expressions: the conjunctions 'and', 'or' and 'if'; the expression of negation 'not'; and the fundamental expressions of quantity (the so-called 'quantifiers') 'all' and 'some'. By applying these logical 'constants' to our essay topics and ringing the changes on their likely combinations, we can develop a number of useful ideas for an essay to explore. In what follows I wish to direct your attention particularly to what can be done with negation (not) and quantification (all, some). It can be very fruitful to ask of the topic, or some part of it, what is *not* the case, as well as what is. And we find, too, that what cannot easily be demonstrated to be universally true of all aspects of the case may be true of *all* aspects of it under *some* circumstances or conditions, of *some* aspects of it under *all* conditions, or of *some* aspects of it under *some* conditions.

An example

> What part did the problems of Central Europe play in the origins of the Cold War?

The one-sentence answer to the question may initially be phrased in such alternative terms as these:

1 Central Europe's problems were wholly responsible.
2 Central Europe's problems played no (significant) part.
3 Central Europe's problems played some part.

Now, these possibilities can be represented in terms of the relations between circles, a representation called 'Euler circles'. The important first step in analysing the topic is to decide how many major terms (or subjects) there seem to be. In this example there seem at first to be two: 'origins of the Cold War' and 'problems of Central Europe'. Each of these terms is represented by a circle, which we shall label *A* and *B* respectively. Our first answer will be represented as in Figure 1: origins of the Cold War and problems of Central Europe are coterminous (*A* = *B*). This means that *all* the problems of Central Europe contributed to the Cold War *and* that there were *no other* causes of the Cold War. The extreme alternative (see Figure 2) is represented as two circles with nothing at all in common: Central Europe's problems and the origins of the Cold War are quite separate issues, so the former can be expressed as a 'not-cause' of the Cold War.

Figure 1   Figure 2

Reflection: asking questions and proposing answers

The general answer that Central Europe's problems played *some* part in the origins of the Cold War can be represented in two quite logically distinct ways with two quite separate meanings. Figure 3.1 means that *all* the problems of Central Europe played *some* part (i.e. that they are a subset of causes),

Figure 3.1

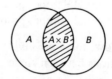

Figure 3.2

while the overlapping circles of Figure 3.2 mean that *some* problems of Central Europe played *some* part but that *some* of its problems played *no* part. Let us, for the sake of illustration, choose Figure 3.2 as the basis of our answer. We are in a position now to see that this gives us at least three related questions to discuss in our essay (A, $A \times B$ and B). A first attempt at an answer might read something like this, in which the three questions are taken up in a sentence each:

> The problems of Central Europe certainly played some part in the origins of the Cold War. However, Central Europe had many problems in these years which had no bearing on the Cold War at all. Moreover, it is arguable that it was not the problems of Central Europe so much as other factors that were central in causing the dispute between East and West.

Now, degrees of 'someness' can be represented in graphic form as in Figures 3.2a, 3.2b and 3.2c and in language in terms such as these:

3.2.a Central Europe's problems played an *overwhelming* part.
3.2.b Central Europe's problems played an *important* part.
3.2.c Central Europe's problems played a *minor* part.

Figure 3.2a

Figure 3.2b

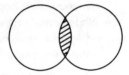
Figure 3.2c

We have so far assumed that the term 'problems of Central Europe' is a simple term. In fact terms consisting of a number of words can be quite complex. It is helpful to analyse this complexity. In the first place, there might be 'problems' that contributed to the Cold War but which have nothing at all to do with Central Europe. What kinds of problem could these be? If they are not problems of *Central* Europe, they could be problems of *other* parts of Europe (north, south, east or west). Similarly, there might be problems not of Central or any other part of Europe but of parts of the world which are not Europe at all (say, the Middle East or Asia). These possibilities for alternative answers can therefore be explored. Finally, if we look at this list of possibly relevant problems,

- Central Europe
- other parts of Europe
- other parts of the world

we can see that they all have one thing in common, namely that they are *regional* problems. Might there be relevant problems which are 'not regional' in nature, but of some other kind?

We are now in a position to propose a second answer. We can give our formal analysis some substance (or content) either by calling on general knowledge or, if this fails, by doing a bit of reading. Using my own general knowledge, I develop the following:

- Problems in the region of Central Europe – as yet I do not need to specify these
- Regional problems elsewhere
  – in Asia, particularly China and Korea

Reflection: asking questions and proposing answers

- in southern Europe, i.e. the Balkan countries
- Non-regional origins of the Cold War
  - the ideological conflict between capitalism and communism
  - the development of nuclear weapons

From this provisional outline the paragraph below can be drafted:

The problems of Central Europe certainly played some part in the origins of the Cold War, though by themselves not an overwhelming one by any means. Central Europe had so many problems at this time that it is not easy to distinguish those that belonged to the aftermath of the Second World War from those relevant to the Cold War. Those that are must be seen in the context of important struggles between pro-communist and anti-communist partisans in other regions, particularly the Balkan states, China and Korea. Furthermore, overlying the problems of Central Europe was a quite separate, though complementary, ideological war of words between East and West. Finally, its problems seem much less startling when set against that major factor in the origins of the Cold War – the nuclear arms race between the USSR and the United States.

There are a few points to make about what we have done so far. First, the paragraph above is not an answer to the question: it is one *proposal* for the *shape* of an answer out of the many that our analysis made possible. (As an exercise you might like to use the analyses above to write a proposed shape of your own.) Secondly, the formal analysis of this topic has enabled us to see that the question could not be answered adequately by confining our attention to the problems of Central Europe. Three other issues have been raised: problems elsewhere, ideological conflict and the nuclear arms race. The analysis also helps us to see that had, say, 'development of nuclear weapons' replaced 'problems of Central Europe' in the topic, the answer would differ more in *emphasis* – including the space allotted to discussing the various origins – than in what is included or left out of the discussion.

To conclude this account of the way in which one can attempt a formal analysis of the possible answers and the shape of those answers, it must be said that this technique lends itself better to some essay topics than it does to others – at least as a way of examining relationships between terms whose relations are to be analysed in the way that 'problems of Central Europe' and 'origins of the Cold War' are placed before us in the topic above. In the topic on General MacArthur, for example, you would need to put forward a number of possible terms (such as we did on p. 35) before you could begin to carry out the analysis of the possible relations between them. Some more sample analyses, including ones on topics of this latter kind, are briefly presented in Appendix 2.

4.4 Evaluative criteria

As soon as you begin to make choices about following one line of enquiry rather than another suggested by your analysis of the topic, you are implicitly making use of certain criteria according to which the choice is made. You saw me doing this in proposing an answer based upon Figure 3.2. No attempt was made at that point to examine *why* I should choose this proposal rather than another. The final stage in your preliminary reflection should therefore be directed towards a consideration of the terms in which your choice might provisionally be justified.

It is useful to begin by asking yourself what you mean by any of the very general evaluative terms thrown up by the formal analysis of relations. In the Cold War topic, for example, it is necessary to ask how terms like 'some part', 'overwhelming part', 'important part' and 'minor part' are to be understood. The proposed answer on p. 46 seems to be assuming that Central Europe's problems were 'not an overwhelming' cause of the Cold War simply because it was just one amongst many others. That is to say, the criterion operating here seems to be based on simple (perhaps simplistic) arithmetic. You will also notice that the 'major factor' in that proposal was judged to be the nuclear arms race, so that by comparison Central Europe was of less importance. To do this, however, is only to shift the problem. By what criterion is the arms race to be judged as 'major'? What is meant by 'major' here? Such general 'quantitative' judgements are certainly necessary; but by themselves they are not sufficient.

Perhaps the most useful strategy in searching for ways of giving substance to such criteria is to try to derive, from either the wording of the topic or the few facts that you have so far assembled, an appropriate 'principle' or a metaphor of some kind. Many, if not most, explanations in the humanities and in the sciences are based on metaphors. War itself is a rich source of them (e.g. cold war, class war, battle of the sexes, war of words, political campaign, capturing the middle ground). By paying attention to the kinds of explanatory principles and metaphors used in the disciplines you study, it is possible to build up almost by second nature a store of approaches to finding suitable criteria to use in your essays.

One way of approaching the Cold War topic is, then, to examine the implications of the term 'war' itself. Ask yourself what conditions are necessary to cause a state of war – hot or cold. One answer to this question must surely be that while wars rarely break out if there are no significant problems in some region of the world, the existence of such problems does not necessarily lead to war. (A more formal way of putting this is to say that such problems are perhaps a *necessary* condition for war to break out, but that they are not in themselves *sufficient*.) Applied to the present case, it will be noticed that the state of cold war did not exist so much between the states of Central Europe themselves as between the USSR and the Western allies. Central Europe just happened to be the battleground on which the giants fought. This is about as far as we need to go in order to attempt a provisional opening paragraph.

5 Drafting a provisional opening

The most fruitful way of revealing to yourself how far your reflection has taken you is to try writing a provisional opening to the essay as early as you can, even though there will necessarily be many gaps of information or analysis that you cannot fill. I think a draft opening paragraph or two is superior to making outlines or jotting down rough notes, since it is only by writing continuous prose that you face the problems of getting straight the RELATIONS between the ideas in your head. Outlines tend to become lists of headings containing only the major issues of content. This can be valuable, but their value lies particularly in sorting out the lengthy main body of the essay. We have not yet arrived at this stage. Our principal aim now is to test the outcome of our early reflections and to give ourselves something that can later be changed and improved upon once the serious reading is begun.

Let us now review the major jobs to be done in coming to terms with a topic before proceeding to apply them. Reflection should yield these things:

- some appreciation of the meanings of the terms used in the topic and the ideas or entities to which they refer, an interpretation of any vagueness or ambiguity in the meaning of the topic as a whole, and just sufficient background knowledge and a few basic categories in which to organise it to get you going (see 4.2);
- a few proposals to examine, arising from the formal analysis of possible relations between the terms (see 4.3);
- a few suggestions as to which criteria might be appropriate to help you decide among the various proposals (see 4.4);
- a decision whether you will answer 'yes' or 'no' to a yes/no question, whether you will agree or disagree with a stated or implied proposition in the topic, or which of the proposals you have developed you will provisionally argue for (see 4.1).

My reflections (which for the present purpose I shall try to make as explicit as I can) on the topic 'What part did the problems of Central Europe play in the origins of the Cold War?' yield these results.

Reflection: asking questions and proposing answers

Meaning and interpretation

'Problems' – political problems or problems of various kinds with political implications; Central Europe – Poland, Czechoslovakia, Hungary, Austria, eastern Germany; 'origins' – interpret this to mean the closing years of the Second World War and the later 1940s; Cold War – the standoff between the USSR on the one side and the USA and its Western allies on the other. The significance of 'what part ... played' categorised initially in broad quantitative terms. No other problems with interpretation.

Proposals

CW's origins solely/partly/not at all due to CE's problems. Eliminate 'solely' since few historical events have a single cause; eliminate 'not at all' since CE is a major frontier in the CW. Now break down 'partly' into 'overwhelming', 'important' and 'minor', and think up (or look up) other possible origins – regional problems elsewhere (especially Far East), nuclear weapons, ideological rivalry between superpowers. Analyse possible relations between these factors.

Criteria

Nature of war in general – between combatants. The main combatants in CW are superpowers, not Central European countries, which at this time had no really effective governments.

Decision

CE's problems important but quite subordinate to the other main factors.

Here, then, is my provisional paragraph:

> The origins of the Cold War are to be found in three major factors: regional problems (both in Europe and the Far East), the ideological confrontation between East and West, and the nuclear arms race made inevitable by the dropping of the atomic bomb on Japan. Of these the second and third were the most important since no state of war – whether 'hot' or 'cold' –

can exist without some conflict of ideology and threat of arms between two belligerents. The problems of Central Europe must be seen in that context. The collapse of the German Reich created a geopolitical vacuum of Central Europe, the countries of which had no effective government. Into this vacuum poured the ideological interests of East and West, symbolised by the 'race for Berlin' between the Russian and Western armies. Poland, Czechoslovakia, Hungary, Austria and eastern Germany were now simply a battleground of the new war to establish viable governments favourable to East or West. Central Europe seems to be important mainly because the action that largely initiated the Cold War – America's use of the atomic bomb on Japan – ensured that there would be no 'race for Tokyo'. At least for a time, superpower confrontation in the Far East was avoided, and attention was free to focus on the rivalry in Europe.

My paragraph might be quite naive (since I am drawing only on my general knowledge) and quite unable to withstand the scrutiny of a tutor in politics. But that does not matter. Just now I am writing not for such a person but for myself, and to illustrate for you some of the processes of reflection I went through.

3
Interpretation: reading and taking notes

> But be ye doers of the word, and not hearers only, deceiving your own selves.
>
> ST JAMES'S EPISTLE

1 The 'problem' of reading

1.1 Common difficulties

Your essay, we found in chapter 2, is *your* 'best' answer to a question. It is not an answer to be found in some book. Nor is it an answer to be found in some combination of books. It is not, on the other hand, an answer to be spun wholly out of yourself as a spider spins its web. The problem of reading for an academic essay is the problem of establishing the relationship between ourselves and our books on a reliable and firm footing. Many students pose the problem in words such as these: 'I know so little about the subject and those who write the books know so much. In addition, these authors express their ideas much better than I can. How, then, can I be expected to give my own answer in my own words when it is all in the books? Much of the time I have to struggle to merely understand what they say, far less give my own ideas.' Put this way the problem is misconceived because such a student sees his or her role as being on the one hand to comprehend and reproduce what the books say while on the other to be 'original'. It is hard to reconcile such extremes. In this chapter the problem will be posed somewhat differently – as a problem not of comprehension, reproduction and 'originality', but as one of INTERPRETATION. Reading is an attempt by you to interpret what a book is saying from your own standpoint and from that of the essay question you are attempting to answer.

If reading is seen thus to be part of a process that includes thinking and writing, you should be able to approach the task in an active frame of mind. Interpreting a book is rather like taking part in a conversation. The reader and the author of the book converse on a subject in which they have mutual, though somewhat varying, interests. Some of the skills you might employ in any conversation which aims at resolving an issue can be brought into play: asking questions of the text, seeking clarification on a point you haven't fully understood, judging the relevance to your question of what the book says, looking for evidence of the author's mood or attitude to the subject, noticing whether and how one thing said squares up with what was said earlier or what was said by another author, and so on. The more thoroughly you have reflected on your essay topic (see chapter 2), the better prepared for interpreting the books you will be, if only because you will have a good stock of questions in your mind and on paper when you go to the library. It is this preparation, and the skills of interpretation to be discussed in this chapter, that should help to give you the independence you will need in order to avoid turning your essay into a pastiche of other people's work.

Such an approach should also help you to cope with some of the other problems of reading:

- How do you stop your mind wandering off on paths of its own, no matter how hard you try to concentrate? By concentrating less on trying to concentrate and giving your attention to your own part in the conversation.
- How do you take notes more efficiently, so that piles of unused paraphrases do not remain when your essay is complete? By constantly interpreting the RELEVANCE of what your sources say in the light of your developing argument for the essay.
- How do you read more quickly? By first of all slowing down and taking the time to build up a general interpretation of what an author is DOING with his text.

Interpretation: reading and taking notes

- How do you get away from the domination of the writer's language over your own? By putting his text away from you and thinking about what he says before you make your notes.
- When should you copy an author's words verbatim into your notes? Not so much when you find an idea very well expressed as when you find something about it that you might want to put under your interpretative microscope in the essay you are planning to write.

It will be the purpose of this chapter to elaborate on these snap answers to some common questions and to put before you some of the various dimensions of interpretation.

1.2 *The importance of background reading*

Textbooks like this one necessarily emphasise the *skills* of reading. It is wrong to get the idea, however, that mastering these skills is all that you require to become a good reader. You will probably notice that you have many more initial difficulties with reading in those disciplines whose content or approach is new to you. Some recent research in reading tends to confirm the common-sense conclusion that the more you know about a subject the easier it is to read in it. The problem, though, is that we usually read academic works *in order to* learn about the content. There is no simple technique that can easily be applied to the solving of this conflict. There is, however, a general programme that you can follow.

The programme is this. You need first to distinguish between the kind of close, critical reading you will need to engage in for your essay-writing and simply beguiling the time with a book because you have a general interest in the subject. Secondly, it is important to give as much time as you can to this general background reading of whole books, and not to confine your reading to poring slowly over the central texts in your course. Both kinds of reading are necessary because they help each other.

General background reading should be done by sitting in an armchair and letting the book wash over you, so to speak, without your stopping to clarify puzzling points, to enquire into the connections between the book and the syllabus, or to assess its relevance to any particular question. What is important in this kind of reading is to grasp the 'plot' and the general rhythm of the exposition, rather as we are commonly supposed to read a novel or watch a movie. If we look for anything in particular, it is only for the beginning, the middle and the end – which is why it is important to read whole books rather than (as our typical essays minimally require of us) just bits of books. A book read in this way can rightly be considered to be as disposable as a late-night television movie or a newspaper article. If there is anything that particularly engages your attention you can mark it or note it briefly on a scrap of paper for *later* critical attention.

Critical interpretation and evaluation such as we use for writing essays feeds on the half-formed images and experiences of general reading. Critical reading must respond to details. General reading gives to these details a context which, though difficult to specify or quantify, enriches them, and over time helps them to make sense. We saw earlier (p. 24) the particular dangers of becoming too 'syllabus-bound'. You can escape these dangers, whilst simultaneously helping your studies, by choosing background reading which is broadly relevant to your course of studies. Many disciplines are now well served by general books for the layman, autobiographies by, and biographies of, significant figures in the advancement of that branch of learning, and some textbooks that are as readable as they are informative. 'Preliminary reading' lists for certain courses are sometimes a guide, and should be treated in the manner suggested above rather than as laborious treatises to be learned. Some publishers have series of very short, inexpensive books on major figures and major topics in particular subject areas which make ideal background reading. Speed, enjoyment, relative superficiality and satisfaction are the criteria which should govern this kind of reading. None of these criteria has of itself any public academic standing. The value of this reading appears only through a crystal lightly in the way you reflect on an essay topic and impart almost unconsciously a richer texture to your writing. Background reading is not time wasted.

2 Evidence, interpretation and fact

2.1 *Primary, secondary and tertiary sources*

Before we can bring tools of interpretation to bear on a text we must first of all decide what kind of text it is and what we hope to gain from it. Some texts contain mostly data. Others contain discussions and interpretations of data, in which the author is arguing for a particular point of view. A third kind of text contains relatively little argument, much presentation of information and few references to the sources of that information.

We shall call these three kinds of text primary, secondary and tertiary sources. Primary sources consist in the object observed; this has to be interpreted by you and by the writers of your secondary sources. They include the poem, novel or play studied by literature students, the documents studied by historians, the painting or the composer's score studied by art critics or musicologists, the 'raw figures' economists analyse, the survey data of the sociologist, the experimental results of the psychologist, and so on. Now, while this seems to be clear enough, the distinction between primary evidence and secondary interpretation does not work so easily in some disciplines. For instance, anthropology students must accept much of an anthropologist's ethnographic data on trust, since the act of recording aspects of a social structure or a custom is itself something of a secondary interpretation on the part of the field anthropologist. Interpretative statements can therefore look very much like statements of fact or pieces of evidence. Even so, it is useful to make the attempt to distinguish where you can.

Secondary sources are the monographs with which the library shelves are mostly filled, and the articles in academic journals and books of 'readings'. It is useful to distinguish two types of secondary source. The first, which we shall call 'theoretical', consists almost entirely of abstract argument which starts from certain premises and argues its way to a conclusion – somewhat like a mathematical proof. The second is 'empirical', and in this case the author takes care to base his arguments on carefully constructed interpretations of empirical data. Such works refer constantly to the primary sources so that the reader can check them out himself if he or she wishes, though they may also have a strong 'theoretical' component.

Tertiary sources, by contrast, are the typical course 'textbook', encyclopaedia, desk dictionary, handbook, etc., which might either be a practical 'how to' book (like this one) or a survey of generally held knowledge in the field. They tend to be based not on primary sources but on secondary sources, and present much of their information dogmatically as received opinion.

Like most boundaries, the borderlines between primary, secondary and tertiary sources can become blurred in certain works. For example, there are textbooks which are very broad in scope but which on some aspects of the subject matter may look very closely at primary evidence and argue for one interpretation of the evidence over others. Similarly, there are often sections in secondary monographs which present information very much in textbook style. In your reading you should watch out for transitions such as these, for reasons we shall go into below.

And again, the same text may fall into two categories, depending on the purpose with which the discipline treats it or on your own particular purpose. An example of this is the status of novels and other works of literature in English and history respectively. In an English course a novel will usually be treated as a primary text. But if the novel contained a portrayal of the life or politics of the times in which it was written, a historian might use it as a secondary source – one writer's interpretation of his times. Even so, if the historian were to switch his interest to the history of contemporary *attitudes* to the government of the day, the novel could then be regarded as a primary source. Plato's *Republic* may constitute a primary source for an essay on Plato, but a secondary source for an essay on theories of government. The issues of interpretation that arise from that same text may therefore vary considerably. This double life is led by many of the classic secondary sources in a discipline: books which were written in order to throw new light on a certain problem themselves become the primary evidence on which later interpretations of their authors' thought are based.

2.2 The consequences of this distinction for essay-writing

To be able to recognise whether, for the purposes of your essay, a source or part of a source is primary, secondary or tertiary will determine how you treat it in your essay. The important question you should always ask is 'Is this statement (or series of statements) a piece of primary evidence, an author's interpretation of the evidence in which the reasoning is shown, or is it authoritative opinion?' Two things follow from this distinction. First, if you have decided that all your essay topic requires is a DESCRIPTION (see p. 28 above), then you can rest fairly content with tertiary sources; if you attempt to justify a point of view (to 'discuss' – as we said most topics require), then secondary and primary sources are critical. Put another way, most academic essays cannot be based upon the reading of textbooks alone. Not only that, but your own essay-writing technique should, in general, be modelled more closely on the way evidence and interpretation are handled in secondary sources than on the style of tertiary texts.

Secondly – and this is of supreme importance because many students have difficulty with it – what is offered as (tertiary) authoritative *opinion* or as *interpretation* in a book should not normally be used uncritically as *evidence* in an essay, unless, of course, you are writing about the interpretations and opinions of the scholars you are examining. Only primary evidence and well-established facts about which there seems to be no debate should be used in this way.* Something of these relationships between you and your sources can be seen in Figure 4.

---

* A fact should be distinguished from primary evidence, though both can be used to build an interpretation on. Facts are really the long-term outcomes of investigations into primary evidence. A fact can be defined pragmatically as a

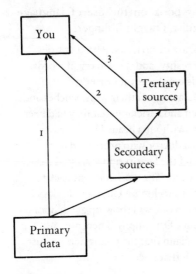

1 Evidence
2 Evidence + interpretations
3 Accepted 'fact' + interpretations

Figure 4

The interpretations and opinions you read should be presented as such in your essay (Smith concludes that..., Smith believes that..., Smith interprets this to mean that..., In Smith's view..., etc.). A writer does not always signal clearly when he or she passes from the presentation of evidence to interpreting or giving an opinion, so you must learn to recognise the implicit signs yourself. Let us examine two short passages.

---

statement (or theory) the truth of which is agreed on by all or most authoritative opinion. Hence it must be distinguished from the authoritative opinion of just some scholars. Not everyone agrees with this definition of a fact, but it does help explain why some of yesterday's 'facts' are today's discarded theories: somebody successfully challenged uniform authoritative opinion. The only sure way to discover whether a statement is truly a fact is to compare several authorities. To take a short cut by relying on a single textbook can be dangerous.

The first is from a popular book on the use of language written by a distinguished linguist, Dwight Bolinger:

> This chapter is about the nature of THINGS. About entities and pseudo-entities. About reality, and the sorcery of words.
>
> On 29 May 1976 the female employees at Carter's Semiconductors in Ipoh, Malaysia, left their workbenches and ran from the factory, terrified and shrieking that they had been molested by a ten-foot ghost without a head. The worried management called in a witch doctor who proceeded to sprinkle rice and water around the factory and sacrificed a goat to appease the spirits of the dead. The workers went back to their jobs and the ghost back to its limbo. Ghosts in Malaysia are a restless lot. Every so often one will show up at a school and frighten the daylights out of the pupils. There are clinical-minded people who claim that the youngsters are just hysterical from overwork, but that of course is pure speculation.

The second paragraph of the extract begins with the recounting of certain facts. Now, since this is not what might be called an 'academic' book, the author does not give the source of these facts, and so we must take it on trust that his version of the story is accurate (and note this in our reference). Everything down to the last sentence, except the interpretative comment, 'Ghosts in Malaysia are a restless lot', will count as fact. The last sentence is, however, interpretative. The author reports other 'clinical-minded' people's interpretation of these events, and then offers his own whimsical and ironic interpretation of their interpretation. Hysteria from overwork is not fact or evidence but, as he says, 'speculation'. That naturalistic interpretation is no less an interpretation than positing the existence of ghosts is: the facts are that these people *said* they saw a ghost; one possible interpretation of this is that they *did* see a ghost.

The second extract is from a book on the psychology of perception. The author, John M. Wilding, is examining theories which attempt to explain how attention works. Psychologists conduct their enquiries by putting hypotheses through various kinds of experimental test. One kind of test designed to study how attention works is the 'dual-task experiment'. Wilding reports this in the first sentence, and we can take it on his authority that such tests are used 'quite widely'. He then goes on – in the way characteristic of disciplines which carry out experiments – to describe an experiment performed by Taylor and to summarise Taylor's results. This is the evidence. In the fourth sentence ('Taylor concluded . . .') Wilding moves away from the evidence and presents Taylor's own interpretation of it. This interpretation is that judgements about whether two lines of digits are the same or different are not performed using the same kind of strategy: one is 'holistic', the other 'serial'. At this point Wilding signals his disagreement with Taylor's interpretation of his evidence, and then goes on to show why he disagrees, offering an alternative explanation:

> Dual processing tasks have been used quite widely to study micro-attention. In an experiment by Taylor (1976) examining letter matching, same–different judgements were made of letters formed out of straight line segments (like those in digital watches and calculators). Same judgements were made equally quickly, regardless of how many segments had to be matched, but 'different' judgements were slower as the number of segments by which two letters differed decreased. Taylor concluded that same judgements were holistic and different judgements were carried out segment by segment. However, it does not follow that the segment analyses were necessarily carried out serially, since clearly if segments are analysed in parallel, completion of one difference signal is adequate to trigger a response. If the time to complete each comparison varies on different trials, then, the more such comparisons are being made, the more likely it is that one will finish quickly and trigger a response. Hence responses will be slower when letters differ by only one segment than when they differ by several. Obviously same judgements could not be explained in the same way, since time to complete analysis of all dimensions would increase as the number of segments to be handled

increased, unless of course extra capacity is deployed for the more difficult task.

This is a good example of a secondary text. There are no assertions or generalisations which are not based on evidence and interpretation. The processes by which Wilding arrives at his own conclusion are spelled out in detail. In writing such as this, however, we are relying on the author to give an accurate summary of the primary evidence – Taylor's experimental procedures and results. We are not given the results in detail. But since there is no question raised about the methods or results, we should probably be justified in accepting Wilding's account. Students of psychology and similar subjects might usefully compare the way in which Wilding constructs this piece of writing with that in which the authors of many introductory texts present received knowledge in the discipline.

Looking thus at the interplay between evidence, interpretation and authoritative opinion in the kinds of source we consult is the beginning of good, critical reading and a sound essay-writing technique.

3 What an author does

There is a kind of note-taking commonly carried out with a finger of one hand on a line of text and the fingers of the other holding the pen on the notepad. The note-taking proceeds a few words at a time, with the eyes flicking from book to pad and back again. This kind of note-taking comes rather close to the 'automatic' response of the copy-typist, who can transfer symbols from one page to another, almost entirely short-circuiting the centres of the brain which process the meaning of the text. Such activity in the library often gives us the sense of being busy, of 'working'. In fact, the productivity of such work is not very high, since sooner or later we are going to have to go through these notes and interpret them. When we do get round to this, we sometimes find that our notes, notwithstanding their faithful rendition of parts of the text, are somewhat incoherent.

We are then placed in the position of having to search out the book again.

Your notes should therefore attempt to be as intelligible an interpretation of the text as you can make them. This means getting away from simply processing the 'surface' of an author's language onto the note-pad. You need to keep up your end of the conversation and to question the text for its meanings. One way of testing whether you have come up with an interpretation of the passage is to put the book from you while you make your note. Unless you have tried (even subconsciously) to memorise the text, most of the words and sentence structures that come to your pen should be your own. If they do not come, either in part or at all, you will need to study the text further – not to memorise but to interpret.

Putting an author's words into your own is called 'paraphrasing', and if you simultaneously shorten the length of the author's text, you are 'summarising' or making a 'précis'. Now, it is important to be aware that the moment you stop quoting or copying the author's words you are paraphrasing, and that every paraphrase you make involves you in the interpretation of the author's meaning. Even in relatively slight changes, a bit of the author is lost and a bit of your interpretation is added. This is inescapable. So it is best to bite the bullet and to begin to see your reading and note-taking not so much as a faithful record of what the author wrote (for which quoting is the only solution) as your considered interpretation of what the author meant. To paraphrase is to make concrete what you think the author means.

If you lack confidence in your ability to interpret an author's meaning without greatly misrepresenting what he or she says, you might need to work quite hard at what is to be said in the rest of this chapter. But if you keep it in mind that your essay is to be *your* 'best' answer to the essay question, you will see it follows that your use of the sources must equally be *your* 'best' interpretation of what they mean. You should try – so far as you can – to make your notes preliminary sketches for some part of the finished essay, just as an artist sometimes makes pencil or charcoal 'studies' of the subject before composing it in paint.

The usual way of representing what the author means is, as we have seen, to paraphrase his or her words in your own. What paraphrasing does is to give your account of what the author is SAYING. The focus is entirely on the content of the author's 'message'. Though necessary, to concentrate exclusively on what the author is saying – on the content – is to miss most of the really important clues that enable you to establish your own 'best' interpretation.

Another way of approaching the question 'What does the author mean?' is to ask what the author is DOING with his or her language. Academic writing (you will remember from chapter 1) does a great deal more than simply try to represent the truth about the subject under scrutiny: a point of view has to be established, the evidence must be assembled and turned into a coherent argument, meanings must be clarified, the reader must be addressed, and the writings of others taken into account. Academic authors will usually be quite explicit about their major aims in the introductory chapter of a book or in the opening paragraphs of a chapter; but not many stop and tell you constantly what they are up to – partly because they themselves are not fully conscious of what they are doing. Good writers (and don't forget that not all academics are good writers) will often litter their text with clues and signposts, but the reader must be able to find and interpret them. Hence it becomes quite necessary to puzzle out what the authors of your books are trying to DO.

You are already familiar with this practice from everyday language. Statements which appear on the surface to be rather similar we easily interpret as DOING different things. When you see on a roadside billboard or in a newspaper

> Fly now, pay later

you will have no difficulty in recognising this to be ENCOUR-AGING or EXHORTING. When you see a rather similar piece of language, say on the billboard outside a church,

Sin now, pay later

you interpret its function to be quite different – WARNING rather than exhorting. You use your experience of the two contexts and your knowledge of language in the word play on 'pay' to ascribe differing functions to these statements.

Similarly, two statements set side by side may in certain circumstances be easily interpreted:

He fell into the river. He got wet.

The first statement EXPLAINS why he got wet, and this causes no difficulty. In

The winter of 1788–9 was a very harsh one in France, inflicting untold misery on the peasants. The Revolution broke out in July 1789.

we might similarly interpret the first statement to be explaining the second, ASCRIBING A CAUSE of the Revolution. But were this to have been written

The winter of 1788–9 was a very harsh one in France, inflicting untold misery on the peasants. Nevertheless, the Revolution broke out in July 1789.

we are immediately faced with a puzzle. Far from ascribing a cause, the first statement is now CONCEDED to be a COUNTER-CONDITION for the outbreak of revolution: perhaps the implication is that miserable peasants turn in on themselves and their problems and are not expected to be found fomenting revolution on the streets. The signal of the change in function from 'ascribing a cause' to 'conceding a countercondition' is contained wholly in the linking adverbial 'nevertheless'. You may speculate what other changes of function and meaning would be signalled by 'coincidentally', 'be that as it may', 'indeed', or even 'for example' or 'incidentally'.

There are three main kinds of motive and intention you need to be able to recognise in order to begin to interpret what an author is doing. The first concerns the author's relationship to other writers; the second the author's ways of analysing the subject matter; and the third the structuring of the subject matter into a coherent sequence of ideas. We shall put them in terms of questions you can ask the text. They are these:

- What is the author's main aim or motive in writing the work (or the part of it in which you are interested) with respect to what others have previously written on the subject?
- What modes of discourse does the writer employ to analyse the subject matter itself, and how is this carried out?
- What does the writer do to structure his or her analyses into a coherent sequence of ideas? How are the parts fitted together in order to compose the whole?

The next three sections of this chapter will examine each of these in turn.

4 An author's major motives

An academic author has to have some overriding reason for putting pen to paper. Some of these reasons will be personal, but they need not concern us. More importantly, the author hopes to make a contribution to an ongoing debate in his or her discipline, and so the work produced must be seen as part of that debate. The major aims of the work will usually be defined in terms of what is already known and thought about the subject and what the writer wishes to add to the work of others. If you look at the foreword or preface to your books you will sometimes find a writer apologising for producing yet another book on the subject, but this apology will quickly be followed by a justification for 'yet another book'.

This justification will usually be worked out in more detail in the first chapter (or, if the work is a journal article, in the opening paragraphs). For this reason, your first task on opening a book is to study the preface and the opening chapter. Only then

should you make use of the index and the table of contents to
hunt down those parts of the work that might be especially
relevant to your essay. The author's major aims provide the
context which enables you to make sense of the detail in the body
of the book, and provide the first clues as to how you will begin
to interpret the substance of what is said. Such discussions, it is
true, are often very general, abstract and theoretical. You might
therefore find them difficult to follow. But some slow, careful
reading here will produce enormous dividends in the speed and
success with which you will be able to read and interpret other
parts of the book. And by the same token, your reading of the
detail will help you understand more clearly those general and
abstract points over which you initially puzzled. (If this sounds
circular, it is. But it is not a vicious circle: the general and the
abstract help you see the significance of the particular and the
concrete, and vice versa.) All academic work demands attention
to both.

The most common motives which govern academic writing
are these:

- AGREEING WITH, ACCEDING TO, DEFENDING or
  CONFIRMING a particular point of view;
- PROPOSING a new point of view;
- CONCEDING that an existing point of view has certain merits
  but that it needs to be QUALIFIED in certain important
  respects;
- REFORMULATING an existing point of view or statement of it,
  such that the new version makes a better explanation;
- DISMISSING a point of view or another person's work on
  account of its inadequacy, irrelevance, incoherence or by
  recourse to other appropriate criteria;
- REJECTING, REBUTTING or REFUTING another's argument
  on various reasoned grounds;
- RECONCILING two positions which may seem at variance by
  appeal to some 'higher' or 'deeper' principle;
- RETRACTING or RECANTING a previous position of one's
  own in the face of new arguments or evidence.

ɔr motives are not mutually exclusive: they can be
in various ways. If we skim through the opening
of Crane Brinton's *The Anatomy of Revolution* (first
ıished in 1938 and revised in 1952 and 1965) we come to this
statement of aims on p. 7:

> Our aim in the following study is the modest one of
> attempting to establish, as the scientist might, certain first
> approximations of uniformities to be noted in the course of
> four successful revolutions in modern states: the English
> Revolution of the 1640s, the American Revolution, the great
> French Revolution, and the recent – or present – revolution
> in Russia. Were we attempting to find an ideal type for
> revolution, were we seeking a kind of Platonic idea of
> revolution, we might be fairly reproached with picking four
> nice neat revolutions which made almost too good a case, too
> perfect a pattern. But we are making no such attempt. It
> should be very clear that not all revolutions, past, present,
> and future, will conform to the pattern here drawn. Our four
> revolutions are not necessarily even 'typical' in the sense the
> word 'typical' has for literary critics or moralists. They are
> simply four important revolutions with which we have chosen
> to begin a work of systematization still in its infancy.

Brinton's main purpose here is to PROPOSE a new way of
studying four famous revolutions of modern times: he is beginning the search for uniformities in them, trying to systematise
the course of these revolutions. Although this aim might not
now seem particularly new, we can infer from his words that in
1938 it was a somewhat novel proposal. But rather than make an
issue of its novelty, Brinton feels the need immediately to
DEFEND it. This he does by REJECTING the likely charge that
he is seeking in these revolutions an 'ideal type' or 'Platonic idea'
of revolution.

Now, you may not know what these two phrases mean. But if
you are to appreciate the significance of what Brinton is proposing, then you must be prepared to find out what it is he is
rejecting. It is the doctrine, associated with Plato, that there are a

few universal laws which determine the underlying pattern of all events (including revolutions) and which humans can do little or nothing to modify. It is the task of the scholar to uncover these laws. This doctrine finds comparatively little favour in Anglo-American traditions of scholarship, hence Brinton's desire not to have his proposal confused with it. Here, then, is an example of the recommendation, made above, that your reading of an author's general aims be slow and as thorough as possible.

We don't have the space to illustrate all the major motives listed above as they occur in the introductory chapters of books. There is, however, an important point to keep in mind, now that we have listed them and asserted their importance for the way you come to terms with a book. It is this. These motives will be found to govern not only whole works, but parts of them, too. Just as it is necessary to identify the major motives of the book as a whole, so it is important to search for them in chapters and in smaller sections of the text. We shall, for example, see various motives in the extract from the body of Brinton's book quoted below.

This extract is taken from the second chapter, entitled 'The old regimes'. In it Brinton analyses those features of the old regimes that made them vulnerable to overthrow by revolution. The part with which we are concerned examines economic weaknesses. As you read it, try to label parts of the text with appropriate terms from the list of motives given on p. 67 above.

> As good children of our age, we are bound to start any such study as this with the economic situation. All of us, no matter how little sympathy we may have with organized Communism, betray the extent of Marx's influence in the social studies – and of the influences that worked on Marx – by the naturalness with which we ask the question: 'What had economic interests to do with it all?'. Since Beard's study of our Constitution, many American scholars have indeed seemed to feel this is the only question they need ask.
>
> Now it is incontestable that in all four of the societies we are studying, the years preceding the outbreak of revolution

witnessed unusually serious economic, or at least financial, difficulties of a special kind. The first two Stuarts were in perpetual conflict with their parliaments over taxes. The years just before 1640 resounded with complaints about Ship Money, benevolences, tonnage and poundage, and other terms now strange to us, but once capable of making a hero of a very rich Buckinghamshire gentleman named John Hampden. Americans need not be reminded of the part trouble over taxation played in the years just before the shot fired at Concord defied all the laws of acoustics. 'No taxation without representation' may be rejected by all up-to-date historians as in itself alone an adequate explanation of the beginnings of the American Revolution, but the fact remains that it was in the 1770s a slogan capable of exciting our fathers to action. In 1789 the French Estates-General, the calling of which precipitated the revolution, was made unavoidable by the bad financial state of the government. In Russia in 1917 financial collapse did not perhaps stand out so prominently because the Czarist regime had achieved an all-round collapse in all fields of governmental activity, from war to village administration. But three years of war had put such a strain on Russian finances that, even with the support of the Allies, high prices and scarcity were by 1917 the most obvious factors in the general tension.

Yet in all of these societies, it is the *government* that is in financial difficulties, not the societies themselves. To put the matter negatively, our revolutions did not occur in societies with declining economies, or in societies undergoing widespread and long-term economic misery or depression. You will not find in these societies of the old regime anything like unusually widespread economic want. In a specific instance, of course, the standard against which want or depression is measured must be the standard of living more or less acceptable to a given group at a given time. What satisfied an English peasant in 1640 would be misery and want for an English farm laborer in 1965. It is possible that certain groups in a society may be in unusual want even though statistically that abstraction 'society as a whole' is enjoying an increasing – and almost equally abstract – 'national income'. James C.

Davies in the *American Sociological Review* (Volume XXVII) suggests that what provokes a group to attack a government is not simply deprivation or misery, but 'an intolerable gap between what people want and what they get', and that revolutions often come during economic depressions which follow on periods of generally rising standards of living.

France in 1789 was a very striking example of a rich society with an impoverished government. The eighteenth century had begun to collect statistics about itself, and though these would not satisfy a modern economist they enable us to be very certain about the increasing prosperity of eighteenth-century France. Any series of indices – foreign trade, population growth, building, manufactures, agricultural production – will show a general upward trend all through the eighteenth century. Here are a few examples: wastelands all over France were being brought under the plow and in the *élection* of Melun alone in two years from 1783 to 1785 uncultivated land was reduced from 14,500 to 10,000 *arpents*; Rouen doubled its production of cotton cloth in a generation; the total French foreign trade had in 1787 increased nearly 100,000,000 *livres* in the dozen years since the death of Louis XV in 1774.

Even in our imperfect statistics we can distinguish short-term cyclical variations, and it seems clear that in some respects 1788–89 was a bad year. It was, however, by no means a deep trough year, as 1932 was for this country. If businessmen in eighteenth-century France had kept charts and made graphs, the lines would have mounted with gratifying consistency through most of the period preceding the French Revolution. Now this prosperity was certainly most unevenly shared. The people who got the lion's share of it seem to have been the merchants, bankers, businessmen, lawyers, peasants who ran their own farms as businesses – the middle class, as we have come to call it. It was precisely these prosperous people who in the 1780s were loudest against the government, most reluctant to save it by paying taxes or lending it money.

Yet the notion persists that somehow or other the men who made the French Revolution must have suffered serious economic deprivation. A very distinguished contemporary scholar, C. E. Labrousse, has sought to prove that there were sufficiently bad price squeezes on little and middling men so that they were spurred to revolution by actual want or at least hardship. Despite his hard work, his general thesis is not wholly convincing. At best, his thesis needs restating along the lines suggested by James C. Davies, and referred to on the preceding page.

In America, of course, with an empty continent available for the distressed, general economic conditions in the eighteenth century show increasing wealth and population, with economic distress a purely relative matter.

Brinton opens his account by ACCEDING to the view that economic factors must be included in the analysis while DIS-MISSING the more extreme Marxist view that economic factors alone can account for revolution. We call this a DISMISSAL rather than a REBUTTAL or REFUTATION since no reasons are offered for rejecting this view: the most Brinton offers is the criterion of the insufficiency of 'only' economic explanations.

He begins the second paragraph not by PROPOSING a point of view, as it might seem to you, but by CONCEDING a particular interpretation of the economic plight of the four countries under examination. What gives away the fact that this is not the proposal for which he will be arguing is the phrase 'it is incontestable that …'. This might look like a very strong proposal. But (like such terms as 'it cannot be denied', 'it is true that', 'certainly', 'manifestly' and 'there is no doubt') in fact it indicates that a major QUALIFICATION is to follow, signalled by a 'however', 'but', 'yet' or similar term. It is this qualification that becomes the main PROPOSAL (or 'main point') in the argument. Therefore, when you read 'it is incontestable that' your eye should begin looking for the 'but' to follow. Brinton supplies it at the beginning of the third paragraph. There he makes his major point by REFORMULATING the original point of view: it is not so much the societies as their governments that are in economic, particularly financial, trouble. Two further examples of this 'yes … but' way of establishing a viewpoint can be seen in the third-last and second-last paragraphs of the extract ('it seems clear . . . however'; 'certainly . . . Yet').

Notice, too, how Brinton deals with a 'no . . . but' in the middle of the second paragraph. Our note could take this form:

> Brinton ACCEDES to the current view which REJECTS the politics of taxation ('alone') as a sufficient explanation of the American Revolution, but QUALIFIES this by insisting on its major importance.

A note of this kind exemplifies the point made on pp. 63–4 above that your notes should try to be preliminary sketches for what you might write in the essay itself.

A final instance of how Brinton positions himself on the controversies surrounding his topic is his DISMISSAL of C. E. Labrousse, advocating that Labrousse's thesis be REFORMULATED on the lines of James C. Davies's, with which he AGREES.

5 Modes of analysis

We turn now from how the author establishes his position in respect of various points of view to the modes in which he analyses the subject matter itself. The fundamental modes of analysis are these:

- THEORISING about and EXPLAINING how or why things are as they are;
- DEFINING terms and concepts by NAMING them, REFERRING to objects, CLASSIFYING individuals into classes, and by DISTINGUISHING between and COMPARING similar classes by means of ASCRIBING characteristics to them;
- DESCRIBING the characteristic features of the objects being enquired into;
- OBSERVING and IDENTIFYING the objects to be analysed;
- EVALUATING the adequacy of our observations, descriptions, definitions, explanations and theories in the light of criteria appropriate to each.

The kinds of statement an author makes in order to analyse the material are the answers to the common kinds of question, set out in chapter 2 (pp. 26–32): 'what', 'which', 'who', 'how', 'why', 'to what extent', etc. The technique to develop for reading and taking notes is the ability first of all to be able to identify which of these analytical modes the author is operating in at any given point in the text and, secondly, to be able to say how the author goes about doing it. Identifying them is not always as easy as it might seem, since there are parts of explanations and definitions of general ideas or concepts that look very like descriptions of particular events or situations. To make judgements about how the author performs these kinds of analysis is a skill that takes some time to build up. It means gradually learning to expect what the main ingredients of, say, an explanation or definition are, and then to measure what the author does against it. This is one of the most important abilities to develop if you want to become a good, critical reader of academic work.

Most of the analytical modes listed above can be seen at work in the second and third paragraphs of the Brinton extract. The second paragraph begins with what we can call an OBSERVATION. Brinton observes a 'fact' about the economic state of the four countries on the eve of revolution. (Notice that this 'fact' is equally an 'interpretation' of the situation being analysed – see p. 59 above.) That this observation is 'incontestable' is not only an indication, as we saw, that it will be qualified. It is also an indication that the author is giving his JUDGEMENT on, or EVALUATION of, its truth, an example of one piece of language performing two separate functions simultaneously.

Having made his observation and given his evaluation of it, Brinton goes on to DESCRIBE the economic circumstances of England under the Stuart kings. Turning to America, he changes his mode of analysis somewhat. Rather than give a similar description, Brinton makes an observation about taxation and then debates whether this is an 'adequate' EXPLANATION of the American Revolution. With respect to France, he EXPLAINS the onset of revolution as the result of the government's calling the

Estates-General to alleviate its financial plight. Then he EXPLAINS why it is that financial collapse in Russia was not so obvious, concluding with a DESCRIPTION of the state of Russian finances, which is offered only implicitly as being also an EXPLANATION of that revolution.

When seen in terms such as these, Brinton's paragraph is something of a mess. England is briefly described without anything much being explained; the American and French revolutions are briefly explained without anything much being described; and Russia gets a bit of each. Were you to be reading further into the chapter, you would need to keep this in mind in order to see whether Brinton makes good these deficiencies. In fact, the fourth and fifth paragraphs of the extract do fill in some of the DESCRIPTIVE detail needed on France.

The third paragraph opens, as we saw, with the main proposal or proposition, couched in the analytical mode of an interpretative OBSERVATION. The rest of the paragraph is largely taken up with a problem of DEFINITION. How is one to define 'economic want'? Brinton refuses to ASCRIBE any of the characteristics of 'economic misery' or 'deprivation' to his definition of want. Indeed, he doesn't really ascribe any characteristics at all to it. Rather, he prefers to define it in relative terms, COMPARING·misery and want in 1640 with its counterparts in 1965 and refusing to DISTINGUISH between them. 'Want', he concludes with the help of Davies, is no more than a considerable gulf between 'what people want and what they get'. The *description* of the French economy in the succeeding paragraphs is intended as a justification of this definition. And his dismissal of Labrousse in the final paragraph is implicitly based on how this historian defines 'want' and 'hardship'.

From this kind of reading it should be clear to you that the various modes of analysis interact in quite complex ways not only amongst themselves but also with the major motives examined in the previous section. To these we must now add a consideration of what the author does to sequence and structure ideas into a coherent whole.

6 An author's structural intentions

The structure of a book is studied by identifying its parts, clarifying the relations between those parts, and understanding the relations between the parts and the whole. The book, as we have seen, will have an overall controlling motive, which is broken down into parts which are usually expressed in chapters which relate to each other in various ways as well as to that overall motive. Similarly, the chapter will have a governing motive, to which its parts – sections, subsections and paragraphs – will contribute. Paragraphs, and even sentences, can also demonstrate these same principles of structure. One of the difficulties of reading any moderately complex work is that of holding together in your mind the very general points whilst simultaneously keeping straight the variety of its detail. Sometimes, there might be little point in worrying too much about the detail, for example when you are doing some background reading, as described on p. 54 above. In reading for an essay, however, you will usually need to fit all the pieces of a text together before you can decide what you need to concentrate on for the purpose of taking notes.

Structuring a text involves you, therefore, in deciding:

- where the author is GENERALISING and where he or she is PARTICULARISING;
- which statements or stretches of text belong together in the ITEMISING of points at any given level of particularity or generality.

Let us make this a little clearer by looking at the Brinton extract. The most general statement is made in the first paragraph – a statement about the importance of economic factors. But this is by way of introduction. His real argument begins with the second and third paragraphs, which are the next most general. A third level of generality is established in the last three paragraphs, which take up the case (or 'example') of France. Knowing, as we do, the aims of the book to be the search for uniformities in the four revolutions, we might predict that this section on France will be followed by a treatment of the other four countries at this level of generality in his argument. This is what in fact happens, as the introductory sentence on America indicates. That is to say Brinton ITEMISES these four countries in establishing support for his thesis. Exactly the same structural pattern of GENERALISATION supported by itemised particulars can be seen within the second paragraph.

The fourth paragraph has four levels of generality. It begins with Brinton's now familiar GENERALISATION in respect of the French economy. In the second sentence the economy is PAR-TICULARISED in terms of 'statistics'. The third sentence makes this more particular still – statistics about certain broad areas of the economy, which he ITEMISES. The fourth, and most particular level in the paragraphs, itemises specific examples of these trends with the 'hard' statistics. This is the most particular level reached by any statement in the extract quoted. The next two paragraphs 'ascend' through the levels to bring us back to the generality of the opening statements of the second and third paragraphs.

You will notice a distinct symmetry in the way Brinton has carried out this structuring of the extract. The general is gradually made more particular up to the end of the fourth paragraph, at which point this trend is reversed. This 'hour-glass' structure is quite a common one and can be looked for in most of the books you read. However, few authors perform it with such transparent precision as Brinton does; so do not expect to be able to structure every text as easily as this one.

There is one final point to be made on the matter of itemi-sation. When you are reading you should always try to give some sort of label to what is being itemised, and to keep a mental count of the items as they come up. The most common sorts of label you can apply are ones like these: facts, factors, features, characteristics, examples, illustrations, cases, reasons, con-ditions, causes, results, arguments, premisses (the statements which, when logically put together, add up to a conclusion), and so on. Assigning labels in this way helps you to distinguish the different levels of generality from each other, and also enables you to make the connections between the elements of structure and the author's analytical modes of discourse. For example, a note on the fourth paragraph could take the form:

> Brinton's DESCRIPTION of the growth in the eighteenth-century French economy ITEMISES three main FEATURES – agriculture (the amount of land under cultivation), manufacturing (cloth production in Rouen) and foreign trade.

The account of an author's motives and intentions given in the last three sections is by no means exhaustive. First, we have said nothing of that aspect of an author's intentions which may be particularly directed at influencing the reader's judgement by means of various rhetorical devices. Nor have we examined the ways in which we can assess the author's own degree of confidence in his or her own arguments. You might, for example, have noticed the extreme 'modesty', even defensiveness, with which Brinton sets out his aims in the paragraph quoted on page 68. We have treated in this chapter only those things which are basic to interpreting a text and taking notes on it.

Secondly, the terminology suggested to you for describing an author's motives and intentions is only a basic vocabulary which seeks to draw your attention to the main things to look for. There are many, many more such words that can be used to talk about what an author is doing. You can build up your vocabulary of such terms best by noticing how the authors of your books use them when they are discussing the work of other scholars. It is here that you will see these terms in action much better than in a textbook such as this. You will also be doing something of great importance: learning to pay attention to academics' language and the way they approach the business of writing academic work.

7 Interpreting a difficult text

The approach to reading and taking notes outlined above is suitable for most books. Brinton is a relatively easy writer to follow, and this approach can be applied without too much difficulty to academic writing of this kind. However, you will at times be faced with texts that you have to labour over in great detail if you are to understand them. These texts are sometimes the 'classics' in your discipline which, because of the quality of their thought, are given considerable attention in some courses. Because of their relative difficulty you might be tempted not to read the texts themselves, but to make do with others' commentaries on them. They can, however, be approached with a bit of work, the rewards of which are inestimable when you come to read the more straightforward works in your discipline. The techniques we have examined remain useful, but now we shall pay much closer attention to individual statements and to the author's use of words. In doing this we can see how, even with very difficult material, we can still bring an author to our own terms and can invest what he or she says with our own personal significance.

Kant's *Critique of Pure Reason* (1781, 1787) is generally reckoned to be one of the more important and, at the same time, one of the most difficult books in Western literature. Still, we can worry at the first three paragraphs of the second edition (1787) as a useful exercise in interpretation. My purpose here is to try to re-create a microcosm of the situation you face when you have difficulty understanding a text and turn to 'secondary' interpretations to help you out. The *Critique* is a 'theoretical' secondary source, as defined on p. 56 above, but one which is nevertheless a primary source for those who wish to understand Kant's thought.

Of the Difference between Pure and Empirical Knowledge

That all our knowledge begins with experience there can be no doubt. For how should the faculty of knowledge be called into activity, if not by objects which affect our sense, and which either produce representations by themselves, or rouse the activity of our understanding to compare, to connect, or to separate them; and thus to convert the raw material of our sensuous impressions into a knowledge of objects, which we call experience? In respect of time, therefore, no knowledge within us is antecedent to experience, but all knowledge begins with it.

But although all our knowledge begins with experience, it does not follow that it arises from experience. For it is quite possible that even our empirical experience is a compound of that which we receive through impressions, and of that which our own faculty of knowledge (incited only by sensuous impressions), supplies from itself, a supplement which we do not distinguish from that raw material, until long practice has roused our attention and rendered us capable of separating one from the other.

It is therefore a question which deserves at least closer investigation, and cannot be disposed of at first sight, whether there exists a knowledge independent of experience, and even of all impressions of the senses? Such knowledge is called *a priori*, and distinguished from *empirical* knowledge, which has its sources *a posteriori*, that is, in experience.

The essence of Kant's distinction between pure and empirical knowledge is summed up in the first sentence of the second paragraph (not, you will notice, from 'there can be no doubt', in the first paragraph). But what does Kant *mean* by the contrast between knowledge 'beginning with' experience and knowledge 'arising from' it? All your note-taking should so far as possible be guided by a question of your own, and this is ours. Below are three quotations from standard commentaries on the *Critique*:

1. It is evident that in point of time all our knowledge begins with experience, but not that it is derived from experience, since the latter may be the indispensable stimulus which moves the mind to an activity of its own. Hence it is important to decide whether we do possess knowledge which is

independent of experience (*a priori*) as distinct from that which is merely empirical (*a posteriori*).   (T. D. Weldon)

2. Kant here lays down his famous principle that all our knowledge begins with experience but does not all arise out of experience, i.e. there is no knowledge temporally before experience but it is not all either causally due to or logically based on experience.* Kant is here using experience to mean sense-experience. Towards the end of the second edition version of the section Kant distinguishes between relatively *a priori* and absolutely *a priori* knowledge, the latter being not merely 'independent of this or that experience but absolutely independent of all experience' . . .   (A. C. Ewing)

* 'Throughout the Introduction the term experience has (even at times in one and the same sentence) two quite distinct meanings, (1) as product of sense and understanding acting co-operatively, and (2) as the raw material (the impressions) of sense' (Kemp Smith, Commentary, p. 52).

3. The argument of Kant's Introduction . . . starts by defining the problem of metaphysical knowledge *a priori*, and through it leads up to the logical problem of the *a priori* synthetic judgement. In respect of time all knowledge begins with experience. But it does not therefore follow that it all arises from experience. Our experience may be a compound of that which we receive through impressions, and of that which pure reason supplies from itself.† The question as to whether or not any such *a priori* actually exists, is one that can be answered only after further enquiry.   (Norman Kemp Smith)

† This statement is first made in the Introduction to the second edition. It is really out of keeping with the argument of the Introduction in either edition. Cf. below, pp. 39–40, 57, 85, 168, 222, 245ff (especially pp. 278, 288).

Each of these three 'note-takers' fixes on Kant's main point – the distinction between knowledge 'beginning with' and knowledge 'arising from' experience. All three note the issue of time in the drawing of this distinction, and also Kant's question whether there is indeed an *a priori* knowledge. Beyond this, however, the differences are considerable. Weldon's seems to me the least helpful because he does no more than merely paraphrase Kant's text. No interpretative comment is offered, such as Ewing does in his text and the footnote, and as Kemp Smith does in his footnote. Moreover, Weldon does not attempt to say what Kant is DOING here, as the others do in their opening sentences. Of the three I find Ewing the most helpful since he does try more explicitly to make sense of the main distinction.

Notice that this does not come from Ewing's own paraphrase of Kant's words. On this score there is little to choose between the three secondary sources:

Kant	begins with . . . arise from
Weldon	begins with . . . is derived from
Ewing	begins with . . . arise out of
Kemp Smith	begins with . . . arise from

None of these variations makes Kant's meaning any clearer to me. Weldon then goes on to introduce the notion of 'an indispensable stimulus which moves the mind' to describe the role of experience. This I find confusing, if not wholly misleading, since I think of a 'stimulus' as a *cause* of a 'response', which is fairly clearly not Kant's meaning. (Weldon was writing in the middle 1950s, when the stimulus–response language of behaviourism was the current fashion.) Ewing's comment indicates that knowledge is preceded by experience in time, but is neither caused by it nor logically based on it.

The next problem is the plethora of terms Kant uses. I cannot be sure about the relationship between knowledge and experience until I am clearer about the meanings of each. It seems from the first paragraph that 'faculty of knowledge', 'understanding' and 'pure knowledge' (in the subheading) are very similar in meaning if not synonyms. None of the commentators helps here (though Kemp Smith uses the 'pure reason' of the book's title); nor does any of them note that Kant suggests that this knowledge is 'within us' (line 9). On experience, Ewing is helpful – quoting a later page of Kemp Smith's book. It seems to me that Kant is using 'experience' in *both* these senses here, 'empirical experience' being defined in his second paragraph. But he uses 'experience', 'empirical experience', 'raw material of our sensuous impressions' and 'objects which affect our senses'. Kant doesn't say so, but the last two may come, not as understanding or pure knowledge does from 'within us', but as impressions on our senses from outside – the external world. I think I can now construe Kant's meaning. My own note on the passage may go thus:

> Kant is attempting to clarify the relative contributions of our experience of objects in the world and a pure 'faculty of knowledge', uncontaminated (as it were) by experience, to our knowledge as a whole.
>
> *Kant's assumption*: we can't have knowledge without first having had experience to 'prime' it.
>
> *Kant's argument*: but to say that e. precedes k. in time is not to say that e. *causes* k. to arise [Ewing], because e. itself may be *partly* supplied by the pure f. of k. or 'understanding' within us. One part of e. – 'raw material' in the outside world acting on our senses – is the part that precedes knowledge. 'Empirical experience', by contrast, is the *product* [Kemp Smith, quoted by Ewing] of our independent understanding (pure k.) acting on the raw material of sense impressions, and in this sense 'arises from' pure knowledge. The pure k. he calls *a priori* knowledge and empirical experience *a posteriori* knowledge. Kant finishes by asking whether it can be shown that *a priori* k. exists.
>
> *Summary*: a latent *a priori* knowledge within us, when incited by raw material from outside acting on our senses, combines with it to produce empirical experience (*a posteriori* knowledge).
>
> NB. This formulation looks like a chemical reaction and Kant uses the word 'compound' (line 13). The *a priori* k. within us must be like a catalyst since it *cannot be changed* by experience – see later in the Introduction.

Well, you say, this is hardly a 'note', since it is almost as long as the original text. But I think any student of literature who has had to write a thousand-word essay on the fourteen lines of a sonnet will sympathise. Where the text is complex, one has to expand before one can produce a summary. Moreover, this note, with appropriate tidying up, could itself be part of an essay. As to the final NB, I have used my more general reading of the Introduction of the *Critique* (the 'whole') to help me see one aspect of the significance of this part, and to justify my own metaphor of the catalyst.

Finally, although I have had to make many judgements in producing this interpretation, I have not given any overall evaluation of Kant's argument – such as the one based on lack of coherence offered by Kemp Smith, itself the result of his wider and deeper reading of the *Critique*. The interpretative judgements I have made are largely, though not wholly, *within* the framework of the three paragraphs quoted – what literary critics call the 'intrinsic' study of the text. This has involved judgements of various kinds:

- how Kant structures his argument;
- how elements of the text function;
- how different parts of the text and the commentaries compare;
- what similarities there are between the meanings of different terms and statements, and what differences of meaning there are in the use of the same term;
- what is *implied* by certain statements (e.g. if pure knowledge is 'within us', sense impressions, by contrast, must come from outside us; if understanding is 'pure' then experience is perhaps 'contaminated' in some sense), and so on.

This last example indicates that I do bring my own language from outside the text to help me interpret it. Other instances are my metaphors of 'priming' (as one primes a pump), and the 'catalyst' in a chemical reaction, for which I seek justification in Kant's own use of the word 'compound'. (Chemical catalysts weren't discovered until nearly forty years after Kant wrote this, so the word was not available to him.) The language of my notes becomes, in effect, a 'compound' of Kant's, the three commentators' and my own – just as each commentator makes a new compound from the elements of his own language and Kant's. In this way one uses the techniques of interpretation to avoid merely paraphrasing the primary text or becoming dominated and confused by the secondary sources. My interpretation is, if not 'original', in important respects my own.

To progress to the highest level of reading by attempting an *extrinsic* evaluation, say, of the justifiability of the distinction between *a priori* and *a posteriori* knowledge as Kant draws it, would mean a lengthy discussion of the *Critique of Pure Reason* and of many other books which tackle not just Kant but the problem of knowledge itself. Such an enterprise we cannot embark on here, but you will see that it would involve similar processes of interpretation welded into the justification of a new argument. That really begins to take us away from the problems of reading proper and back to those of writing.

Part II

The
Dynamics
of
an Essay

4
Openings

> A speech has two parts. You must
> state your case and you must prove it.
> You cannot either state your case and
> omit to prove it, or prove it without
> first having stated it; since any proof
> must be a proof of something and the
> only use of a preliminary statement is
> the proof that follows it.
>
> ARISTOTLE

1 The constituents of an essay

What Aristotle has to say about a speech applies equally to a modern academic essay: the opening states your proposition or answer, and the body of the essay justifies that answer. Our study in chapter 2 of the ways in which you can reflect on your essay topic has already prepared you for the writing of your opening. In this chapter we shall say more about how you can establish your case. Chapter 5 will take up the problems of justifying or demonstrating that case. In chapter 6 we learn how to write that part of an essay which Aristotle thought only an optional element, the conclusion or end.

We shall think of an essay, therefore, as a structure with an opening, a middle and an end. The opening states your case, the middle justifies it and the end reflects on the beginning and the middle. Within this broad structure there are quite a few elements which also have to be taken into account, fitted together and turned into a coherent unity.

These elements are set out below. As you study them, bear in mind particularly that this list is not a sequence of stages in the setting-out of an essay. Nor is it an ordered formula which you can apply in a uniform manner to every essay you write. The discipline in which you are writing, the essay topic itself and the nature of the answer you decide to give will all affect which of the elements you emphasise, how you will treat them and where in the essay some of them will be introduced. The relations between the elements in this list can be quite complex, so do not try to oversimplify them:

- an interpretation of the question if you find it ambiguous, vague in some respect or rather open-ended, and, where relevant, such introductory material as a clarification of the meaning and significance of any important terms or 'background' necessary to the establishing of your proposition;
- a proposition (or a series of propositions) with whatever qualifications and conditions you deem necessary to defend it, which formulates your 'best' answer in language as clear, precise and economical as you can muster;
- an account of the evidence and interpretations on which you have chosen to base your proposition: evidence may consist of facts, primary data, descriptions, or generally accepted definitions; interpretations will consist of the connections (explanations, theories) to be made between them;
- an account of the evidence (facts, descriptions, etc.) which 'best' tells against some aspect or aspects of your argument, CONCEDING its force where necessary, CRITICISING it where you can, and INTERPRETING it in such a way that your original proposition is left substantially intact;
- an evaluation of the strengths of your argument and evidence (and the counterarguments and counterevidence) by reference to appropriate criteria;
- a demonstration of how your chosen approach has been RELEVANT to the question with which you began – for the essay as a whole, for some section of it, or for some paragraph;
- a concluding reflection on some aspect of your answer.

If all this is going to work well, we shall need to pay particular attention to the writing of our opening since it is there that the 'golden thread' which makes our argument RELEVANT and COHERENT is crafted. So we shall now take up the first and second of the elements above.

2 The constituents of an opening

We shall call the start of an essay a 'beginning' or an 'opening' rather than the usual 'introduction'. For many students an introduction suggests a discourse on the background to a topic, a definition of terms, a setting of the scene, or attention to some other set of preliminaries to the essay proper. An opening may well include various of these things, but not at the expense of coming to grips with the essay topic itself: stating your case is the fundamental function of your beginning not only because readers tend to look for such a statement but also because it is here that the RELEVANCE of your answer to the question and the COHERENCE of your argument are first established. A relevant and coherent beginning is perhaps your best single guarantee that the essay as a whole will achieve its object. That is why your opening – of all parts of the essay – needs the most careful consideration and the most frequent rewriting.

The only necessary constituent of an opening is, as we have seen, a statement of your case. This statement will typically take the form of an *answer* to the question (or implied question) contained in the topic. But once an answer is given, it tends to beg another question: what are the reasons for your answer, or (which may often amount to the same thing) what are the criteria according to which you have made your judgement. This, in turn, may suggest yet another constituent of an opening. If we make a judgement, the implication is that we have decided in favour of one answer (our 'best' answer) over alternative answers – we have made a *choice*. Consequently, we might expect that our opening will either indicate the nature of that choice or convey in some way the confidence the writer places in the adequacy of either his own or another's answer. In other words the opening should express your 'motive', as this term was developed in the previous chapter (see p. 66). It can say what point of view is being PROPOSED or ACCEDED TO; it can say what point of view is being CONCEDED subject to certain QUALIFICATIONS or EMPHASES the writer wishes to high-light, or how that point of view can be REFORMULATED to make it acceptable; or it can say what in that point of view or in others is being REJECTED. Only RECANTATION is inappropriate in a student's essay, since a recantation implies that you have written and published on the subject before.

These seem to be the important constituents of an opening. As we have seen, it may also include relevant 'introductory material' if it seems called for. Finally, an opening may indicate the lines on which the main body of the argument is to be conducted.

All this makes rather severe demands upon the writer of an opening. To know *what* the constituents of a good opening may be is one thing. To know *how* they can be integrated into an effective opening is quite another. There is no system of rules to follow in constructing an opening. But this is not to say that *any* structuring of the constituents will produce a relevant, coherent and forceful opening to the essay. The nature of the constituents themselves will place certain constraints on how they can be used. The art of composition is, then, to take them and create variations of form in response to differing kinds of essay topic, differing disciplinary traditions and the differing demands of the subject matter itself and the emphasis or prominence you wish to give to certain aspects of your answer.

To summarise. The basic constituents of the opening to a discussion are

- an answer to the question (or implied question) raised by the essay topic;
- a set of reasons for your answer, or an indication of the criteria according to which your judgement has been made;
- an indication, in respect of your answer, of any qualifications you wish to make, conditions you need to impose, emphases you want to place, or of any concessions to, reformulations of, or rejections of, other possible answers.

Other constituents of the opening may include:

- introductory material relevant to the case you are putting forward;

✗ • an indication as to how the main body of the justification will
    be approached.

Our plan will be, so far as is practicable, to build up a series of
openings in which various of these constituents are highlighted.
(These are given as examples 1–6 on pp. 96–105.) This is not to
say that later versions of our opening are necessarily a cumula-
tion of all the virtues of the earlier ones. In taking one tack we
often lose some of the advantages of another. In opting for a
more complex opening we sometimes have to sacrifice some of
the virtues of simplicity. With the exception of (2) (see p. 96),
which was written by a student, I have composed all the
examples for the present purpose.

We shall begin by examining the misuse of introductory
material. Then we shall go on to see how the basic constituents
of an opening may be built up. Finally, we shall see how optional
introductory material can be accommodated in an opening that
does answer the question.

3 The use and misuse of introductory material

Having reviewed the circumstances in which various kinds of
'introduction' are appropriate, Aristotle observes:

> Introductions are popular with those whose case is weak, or
> looks weak; it pays them to dwell on anything rather than the
> actual facts of it. That is why slaves, instead of answering the
> questions put to them, make indirect replies with long
> preambles.

The usual function of an 'introduction' in academic writing is to
tell the reader what issue is being raised and what justifies the
writer in raising it – for example, that it has been neglected, that
new evidence has come forward, that previous writers have
misinterpreted some aspect of it, that there is a gap in our
knowledge, that a new theory or approach throws a different
light on well-known facts, and so on. You will see this kind of

introduction in the articles to be found in academic journals and in the preface or introduction to a book. For the most part it is not appropriate to an essay in answer to a question set by your tutor, since you need not offer the reader an excuse or a reason for taking up the matter. The essay topic raises the issue, and since both writer and reader share their knowledge of this context nothing is to be gained by justifying why you have taken it up. Aristotle's slaves are expected to answer the question put to them without preamble. So is a student. Only where you have formulated your own essay topic is an introduction which fulfils the functions described above strictly necessary.

This is not to say, however, that no material which might be considered introductory to the main argument should be included in your opening. It may, just so long as it does not *replace* the essential feature of that opening, a statement of your case. If there is no reason for having to announce the issue or why it has been raised, there is often, nevertheless, good cause to indicate *how* it can be tackled. Some essay topics are either ambiguous in meaning or very general in scope, such that the essayist needs to say how he or she has interpreted it, and further, to say *why* this interpretation is a fruitful one. It might be that you suspect the answer will not be as obvious as it appears on the surface, that it has implications beyond the immediate problem, that you are aware of significant new evidence which might suggest a revised interpretation of the problem, that it throws up an interesting methodological issue, and so on. In such situations you need to inform your reader how you have interpreted the topic, what it is you find interesting in your question, and what needs to be concentrated on to answer it.

We studied such a case in chapter 2 (p. 39): 'Why was George III accused of attempting to subvert the constitution?' An interpretation that seems interesting because it may have implications beyond the obvious problem would be to examine the motives both of his contemporary accusers and of later historians and politicians who had a particular dislike for the King. I think the interest of this interpretation lies in the fact that it raises questions about how the reputations of historical figures become established and perpetuated. So my opening would introduce these issues *as part of* the case for which I propose to argue rather than as a wholly separable 'introductory' section.

Any such introductory material should, as far as possible, be thus integrated into some aspect of your statement of the case. The criterion to be employed in choosing and integrating this material is its RELEVANCE to your case. There is no point in 'defining your terms' unless your case is going to hinge in part upon the definition (or interpretation) you give of a term. 'Background material' (historical, biographical, geographical, sociological, cultural, etc.) must similarly be selected for its relevance, or passed over so quickly as not to disturb the reader's concentration on the case you are putting. The opening to an essay on the effect of the environment on the social organisation of the Kalahari bushmen may well need to notice relevant geographical features of the Kalahari desert where they live. By contrast, one on the structure of their myths would leave these factors out unless their relevance can be suggested. Similarly, the facts that the German composer Wagner would wear nothing but silk and satin next to his skin and that he needed a special preparation of attar of roses to inhale as he worked, might be a trivial distraction to one essay opening. In another, it might be a succinct way of making concrete and objective a case about some qualities of his music. Introductory observations are thus not so much a means by which you ease your way into the main issues of the essay. Rather, they are a necessary or arresting adjunct to the formulation of your point of view on the topic, or an indication of the scope within which the discussion of the issues will take place. We shall examine later some of the ways in which introductory material can be deployed.

But first we shall exemplify an opening which, however suitable in a textbook, really has no place in an essay. The topic we shall take in all the examples that follow is 'Account for the failure of Chartism'. The preamble below makes no case and barely glances at the question underlying this topic.

I

The Chartist movement began in the 1830s as a working man's
response to the economic, social and political problems
generated by the industrial revolution in England. As a
political programme it was a revival of the radical tradition of
the eighteenth century, which had raised the cry of manhood
suffrage. There is also something of the tradition of the
seventeenth-century 'levellers' in their programme, and it has
even been claimed that the idea of a people's charter had its
origins in Magna Carta. The Charter itself was published by
the London Working Men's Association in 1838, and it called
for 'universal suffrage, no property qualification, annual
parliaments, equal representation, payment of members [of
Parliament] and vote by [secret] ballot'. The Chartist
movement died out in the 1850s after a good deal of violence
and the failure of its mass demonstration at Kennington
Common in 1848, without having achieved its object. It was
yet another example of the failure of radicalism in England.

4 Setting out your case

We shall now begin to build up a few openings that do set out a
case. At first sight (2) looks as if it is answering the question, but
in fact what we have here is really only the raw material on which
an answer could be based. There is no emphasis, nor any indication of a controlled interpretation of the causes of the failure of
Chartism.

2

From the evidence available I have come to the conclusion that
the Chartist movement failed because of (a) bad organisation,
(b) personal and sectional differences, (c) growing power of
the Anti-Corn Law League and the revival of trade unionism,
(d) geographical divisions, (e) inferior weapons and means of
communication, (f) failure with its petitions and with the mass
demonstration, the 'fiasco of Kennington Common', (g) the
strength of the middle classes rather than the weakness of the
uneducated and poorly organised working classes, (h) govern-

ment repressive measures and (i) the mere fact that because it failed in London, it did not leave hope for success elsewhere.

But this paragraph can be rescued. A little reorganisation of the items in this shapeless list will reduce these 'causes' to a few major ones, for example:

(i) poor organisation and leadership (a, b, d, e, f, i);
(ii) the entrenched power of middle-class opposition as found in the Anti-Corn Law League and middle-class support for government repression of the Chartists (c, g, h).

But in rewriting the paragraph we do a little bit more than just categorise these causes. We must replace the rather elementary organising principle of conjunction ((a) *and* (b) *and* (c) *and* (d), etc.) with something that will show more interesting relationships between the facts in the list. In the paragraph below this is done in two ways. First, a choice has been made as to which the more 'underlying' causes of the failure of Chartism are (i.e. (i) and (ii) above), such that we now have a certain 'hierarchy' of causes: some things flow from others. Secondly, another major relationship has been introduced in order to bring (i) and (ii) under a single umbrella. This relationship is that of conflict between the working-class Chartist movement and the middle-class supporters of the Anti-Corn Law League. This conflict suggests to me, furthermore, that I can CONTRAST the two movements. Most of the information in (2) has been retained:

3
The Chartists failed because their education, experience and ability to organise were no match for the combination of conservative middle-class forces ranged against them. Personal and factional rivalries within the movement hindered the spread of a common strategy throughout the country, with the result that it never captured any real support in the place where such support was most needed – London. By contrast, middle-class opposition to the Chartists was capably organised by the Anti-Corn Law League, who made such skilful use of

> their London contacts and their publications that the
> government were in no doubt that repressive measures against
> the Chartists would be generally approved. The 'fiasco of
> Kennington Common' shows how all these things came
> together and spelt the eventual end of Chartism.

When they are analysing causes, many historians and others feel what E. H. Carr calls a 'professional compulsion' to try to decide which cause or group of causes 'should be regarded "in the last resort" or "in the final analysis" ... as the ultimate cause, the cause of all causes'. Not everybody agrees with Carr in this matter, but it is undeniable that the desire to tie heterogeneous things up in a 'unified vision' exerts a powerful influence on the academic imagination. In (3), as we have noted, the unity is secured by interpreting the failure of Chartism as a lost battle with the middle-class Anti-Corn Law League.

You may often find, on the other hand, that the essay topic you are writing on, the subject matter itself or certain methods of analysis in particular disciplines precludes this kind of unity of explanation. For example, a statistical factor analysis of many variables in psychology or economics might produce a number of factors which cannot be reduced any further. A linguist might be forced to conclude that there is no single set of grammatical rules which can account for the variability in usage to be found in different speech communities. Even so, we will usually feel that nothing much has been EXPLAINED if we finish any work with a long list of unrelated or loosely related factors such as we saw in (2).

So, where you are not able to establish 'in the final analysis' a wholly unifying interpretation, you should still feel a 'compulsion' to reduce the list of issues, factors, reasons, causes, 'aspects', variables, categories, or whatever they may be, as far as you can. The number that suggests itself to me is three or four. While it does not constitute a reason for fixing on these limits, the fact that in English we routinely say 'firstly', 'secondly' and 'thirdly', rarely 'fourthly', and never 'fifthly' unless we are having a joke, might be taken as informal corroboration. (In place of 'fourthly' we might speak of a 'penultimate' factor, and for the last we usually say 'finally'.) There will be exceptions, such as those noted above, but I recommend that you think very carefully before allowing the factors underlying the organisation of your answer to multiply beyond four.

The core of a 'discussion': debating your answer

The kind of answer exemplified in (3) is certainly adequate for many purposes. It is reasonably well UNIFIED and it embodies a JUDGEMENT on why Chartism failed – it puts forward a case, as Aristotle says it should. But what it lacks is a sense of self-awareness, an awareness that comes from the recognition that this may not be the only answer, and that, even if it is the 'best' answer, there might be some important considerations that have been neglected or pushed aside in its desire to be forceful.

If you look at that opening carefully you will see that it does not explicitly advance any REASONS for the interpretation it offers. It does, of course, advance reasons for the failure of Chartism, but that is a different matter. What we are looking for now is a reason why the PROPOSITION that Chartism was defeated by middle-class opposition to it should be accepted. Opening (3) only gives plenty of SUPPORT to the proposition announced in the first sentence. For the opening to be self-aware it needs to be aware of other interpretations or, at least, of certain shortcomings in itself which might raise the possibility of other interpretations or judgements. A judgement, in the words of the literary critic F. R. Leavis, implies more than just the statement of a (private) proposition:

> the implicit form of a judgement is: This is so, isn't it? The question is an appeal for confirmation that the thing *is* so; implicitly that, though expecting, characteristically, an answer in the form, 'yes, but –' the 'but' standing for qualifications, reserves, corrections. ('Two cultures?' The significance of Lord Snow' in *Nor Shall My Sword*)

The answer to Leavis's question might equally be 'no, but –', in which the respondent disagrees with the proposition while finding certain things in it to be commended or conceded. Our fourth opening will try to convey this sense of a discussion:

4

Chartism, it appears, failed for some combination of two main reasons. First, the movement was never an effective political force: it was poorly led and divided both in its aims and over the means by which those aims were to be achieved. Although its platform was one of parliamentary reform – as set out in the six points of the People's Charter – it concentrated its tactics on bread-and-butter issues, about which the diverse elements of the working classes at the time could not agree. Secondly, the lack of Chartist unity was exploited by the middle-class adherents of the Anti-Corn Law League, who had an interest in preventing their own political power from becoming diluted and (it has been claimed) in using free trade to keep down working men's wages.

However, it is unlikely that any such movement as Chartism, no matter how well organised and no matter how effectively it had managed to cooperate with the middle classes, could have succeeded in the early period of nineteenth-century industrial growth. Although the rhetoric of 'the working classes' was strong at the time, industrial capitalism had not by the 1840s advanced to the stage where it had created throughout Britain a dependent, uniform working *class* as a socio-economic formation. That was to come later. Chartism failed not just because of poor strategy and tactics and of middle-class opposition, but because as a political movement it was premature.

In this opening most aspects of the answer contained in (3) are accepted, but found to be insufficient. It CONCEDES that poor organisation and middle-class opposition were vital factors. The awareness that this is not the whole story turns on the 'however' beginning the second paragraph, a foretaste being signalled by 'it appears' in the very first sentence of the opening. Hence running through this opening is a dichotomy between an appearance and an underlying cause which is responsible for the appearance. This argument, you will notice, was only made possible by posing a 'negative question': 'Would Chartism still have failed if the conditions set out in (3) had *not* prevailed?' The answer is 'probably yes'.

Because our essay topic is phrased as an open-ended instruction ('Account for the failure of Chartism'), it was necessary to go through the stage of analysis represented by (3) before an opening like (4) became possible. Often, of course, the essay topic itself will help you through this preliminary stage. Such is the case when it includes a proposition to be discussed: '"Chartism was doomed by its poor organisation and the hostility of the Anti-Corn Law League." Comment.' Once you have a provisional answer in a form such as this (whether supplied by the tutor or laboriously assembled from the sources by yourself) you are in a position to reflect upon its adequacy. At this point you can simply ACCEDE TO it (as in (3)); you can CONCEDE that it has a certain adequacy as an interpretation but that you need to attach certain QUALIFICATIONS, CONDITIONS or REFORMU-LATIONS before you accept it (as in (4)); or you can REJECT it, giving your reasons – what is called a REFUTATION ('Chartism failed not because of poor organisation and middle-class opposition but because . . .').

'But', 'however' and 'yet' are the workaday signals of QUALI-FICATION, along with the stronger 'nevertheless', 'even so', 'notwithstanding', 'despite this', 'in spite of this', and so on. As we saw in chapter 3, the proposition or preliminary statement makes the point to be CONCEDED, and the linking terms above introduce the qualification. (With 'although' and 'even though' the reverse applies: these conjunctions introduce not the quali-fication but the point to be conceded, for example, 'Although the failure of Chartism can be attributed in part to poor organisation and middle-class opposition, the main cause was the lack of working-class solidarity.') Here are some examples of the ways in which these phrases can be used:

> This description characterises the situation in certain societies well, but it does less than justice to what is observed in society X and society Y.
>
> The programme was a success, but only insofar as it achieved a limited set of goals.
>
> The considerable support we find for this interpretation notwithstanding, it is still necessary to point out that ...
>
> It can hardly be denied that X is ... Even so, this does not account completely for the fact that ...

Notice how many of these examples are thick with functional terms referring to what scholars (or their writings) DO: characterise, observe, support, find, interpret, point out, deny, account for. The use of such language is a correlate of that 'self-awareness' of a good opening (or much good academic discussion) we spoke of earlier.

Closely related to concession and qualification, though serving a slightly different function, is the imposition of certain CONDITIONS upon your acceptance of a proposition. The problem with conditions is that there is a danger the whole question will be begged. For example, when asked to say whether marriage is a universal human custom, we might decide that it is, *provided that* our definition of marriage dispenses with criteria which prevent it from encompassing certain difficult cases. To accept woman-to-woman 'marriage' among the Nuer in southern Sudan as marriage would be to impose the condition that marriage need not be heterosexual. To accept the customs followed by the Nayar of southern India, which allow a woman many sexual partners, would be to impose the condition that marriage is not necessarily an institutional means of establishing the legitimacy of children. The obvious retort to such arguments is that the set of criteria we adopt to define marriage is precisely the point that needs to be discussed in the body of the essay. To set conditions such as these is to avoid discussing it. Nevertheless, where a discipline conventionally adopts certain conditions (such as the *ceteris paribus* clause – 'other things being equal' – in economics) we can with care formulate cases such as these:

This is true provided that we confine our attention to . . .

The reasons are . . . only if we accept that . . .

Here is an example of one such approach to the question on Chartism:

5

If the success of radical protest movements depends principally upon the political acumen and experience of their leaders, then the Chartist movement failed because of indifferent leadership. Regional rivalries amongst the leaders, failure to enforce a disciplined common strategy, too much concentration on side issues and the turning of the Anti-Corn Law League into an enemy all demonstrate political naivety in the Chartist movement. There are broader issues beyond these very concrete ones which may also have contributed to its failure. For example, the workers on whom it depended for support had not yet developed a united class consciousness. Nor was the economic climate so continuously bad that support on 'bread-and-butter issues' could be relied on. Even so, Chartism was first and foremost a protest movement, so its failure must be judged in the day-to-day political terms of such movements.

This opening makes the answer conditional on our accepting two things. The first is the truth of the proposition that 'the success of radical protest movements depends upon the political acumen and experience of their leaders'. The second, which is implicit in this statement but made quite explicit in the final sentence, is the STIPULATION or ASSUMPTION that Chartism is best thought of as a 'protest movement' rather than as some other kind of political force. Hence the criteria by which such movements must be judged are those of everyday practical politics rather than the grander or more abstract criteria used in the second paragraph of (4).

It is, of course, open to a reader to dispute the two conditions that have been made in (5). For this reason a good opening would go on to 'clear' this ground by dealing as briefly as possible with the reasons for regarding the Chartist movement as a protest movement and no more. Chartism was not, it might be summarily argued, the conception or birth of what was to become the Independent Labour Party in England. Any such opening that relies heavily on conditions or definitions that could be challenged will need to be expanded upon in a few ground-clearing paragraphs. This consideration brings us back to the ways in which various kinds of introductory material can be incorporated into the case you wish to establish in your opening.

Integrating background material

The openings to our essay on Chartism (2), (3), (4) and (5) are very spare. They seek to get straight to the point in their desire to avoid the 'background' irrelevancies of (1). Our final example attempts to integrate into the answer some of the concrete historical facts which both 'set the scene' and help the argument along (notice how many dates are given). By quoting from contemporary sources, it also tries to convey something of the flavour of the period. Finally, it seeks simultaneously to present an argument and to include a few elements of narrative. I rather like this attempt to make the argument more concrete, but my preference may not be shared by all readers:

6

'I defy you to agitate a fellow with a full stomach.' William Cobbett wrote this in 1836, the year in which one of the earliest of the many diverse Chartist organisations – the London Working Men's Association – was founded. Of the ensuing twelve years up to the fiasco of Kennington Common only half (1837–42 and 1847–8) were lean years for the working man. The Chartist fortunes fluctuated accordingly, and finally dissolved in the prosperity of the 1850s. The movement's misplaced reliance on 'hunger politics', moreover, made it difficult to

convince even many working men that, as one leader claimed,
'this question of Universal Suffrage was a knife and fork
question after all'. The connection was never obvious, and in
attempting to make it the disunited and poorly organised
movement never obtained a sufficient degree of class and
national solidarity. But if there was any single major error of
judgment, it was in rejecting the compromises necessary to
gain middle-class support. Chartism was in turn rejected by a
class whose own enfranchisement in 1832 and whose victory
over the Corn Laws in 1846 allied it with a government
determined to have no 1848 revolution in Britain.

It will be left to you to compare both the content and the
method of treatment of this opening with the earlier ones. We
shall close this chapter with one observation. None of the
beginnings illustrated above has explicitly told the reader how
the argument in the main body of the essay will be organised.
There are no statements to the effect that 'we shall first investi-
gate such and such and then turn our attention to this and then
that'. For the most part, an essay (unlike a longer work) can
eschew such explicit guidance to the reader in its opening, if the
opening is composed in such a way that it models both the
argument and the sequence of issues to be taken up in the
middle. If an opening is thus a microcosm of the essay as a whole,
there should be no need to address your reader directly about the
order in which you propose to deal with your material.

5
Middles

His knowledge is extensive, various,
and profound. His mind is equally
distinguished by the amplitude of its
grasp, and by the delicacy of its tact.

MACAULAY, OF HALLAM'S
Constitutional History of England

The middle of your essay is the opening writ large. Its underlying constituents will therefore be quite similar to those
studied in the previous chapter. But there is in the middle a
major shift of emphasis away from bald propositions and conclusions towards the careful working-out of arguments and the
balancing of interpretations with the evidence you call upon to
support them. To justify the case presented in your opening is to
develop arguments, to deploy evidence, to evaluate the strength
of counterarguments and apparent counterevidence, and to
demonstrate their relevance to the question with which you
began. In all this your aim is to show not so much that the
answer you have decided on is the right answer, but that it is a
reasonable point of view to hold.

If the process of writing always went ideally according to plan,
then the crafting of a good opening should forestall most
(though not all) of the difficulties one might otherwise encoun-
ter in writing middles. But just as you need to get an opening of
some sort written to help guide the argument of your middle, so
you might often find that problems encountered in the writing
of the middle lead you back to a reconsideration of your
opening. The opening should never be regarded as finished and
out of the way until you are satisfied that you cannot fundamentally improve the argument of your middle and that your
middle justifies the case put forward in the opening as well as you

can make it do so. If you get stuck at some point in the writing of the middle, it is often, therefore, a good idea to hunt for the source of the difficulty in the opening itself or in the analysis you carried out in preparation for drafting it (see chapter 2).

In this chapter we shall examine some of the common problems encountered in the writing of middles and suggest ways in which they can be solved. They include changing your mind about the answer, grinding to a halt having lost the thread of ideas, writing too much, writing too little, and structuring the essay. Then we shall go on to study more closely some of the issues peculiar to middles themselves: principally the elaboration of a point into an argument, dealing with the differing opinions often to be found in your books, and the ways in which evidence is brought into play. These matters are closely associated with the ways in which we structure our paragraphs and groups of paragraphs.

1 Some common problems

1.1 Changing your mind about the answer

There are times when even the most careful preparation might seem to be mocked when you discover half-way through the writing of the middle that you have quite changed your mind about the case set out in your opening. This can happen because it is only in the grappling with details of argument and evidence necessary to a middle that the full significance of something strikes you. (Remember that it is often in the act of writing itself that new knowledge and new interpretations of evidence are created.) When this happens the first thing to keep in mind is that it is no disaster – unless you have left the writing until a minute or two to the twelfth hour. First, you must convince yourself that you really have changed your mind, and not just come to doubt the degree of your commitment to the case you have been making. If this doubt is not too great, it might be possible to accommodate it in the conclusion to your essay (see pp. 132–3 below). Secondly, having decided to change your case, you must accept that revisions to your previous work will have to be made, since it is not acceptable to submit an essay that changes its argument half-way through. This does not mean, however, that you must begin all your work from scratch. It means that you will have to go through what you have written, reinterpreting the facts you have assembled in the new light and modifying the point of view on the arguments set forth. This might involve no more than, for example, elevating what previously seemed a minor point to major status or CONCEDING that what seemed before to be a major argument is now only a QUALIFICATION to another argument. But before making any changes to the earlier parts of your middle, always try rewriting the opening to test whether you have got your new argument sufficiently straight in your head.

1.2 Grinding to a halt

Many academic writers find that no matter how carefully they have prepared the ground in advance, they sometimes come to a stop, and there sets in a 'writer's block' that owes less to doubts about what they are writing than to the elusiveness of an argument or thought that is being developed. The thread that was being followed or grasped at is lost.

- Sometimes this block can be overcome by rereading from the beginning of the section on which you are working in order to catch the drift of your ideas.
- At other times you may need to scrutinise the main point of the section quite closely: the problem might lie in the way the initial point was formulated either in the opening or in the section of the essay that takes it up. There might be an unintended emphasis, an ambiguity, a confusion, or some other problem in your expression of the point, which led you astray.
- If you find nothing of this kind, it sometimes helps to go into something like a trance, in which you try to recapture the

essence of what you were trying to say (a kind of mental correlate of attempting to grasp a word on the tip of your tongue).

- If these strategies fail, it is often a good idea to leave your desk for a while and do something quite different: the resolution of the difficulty has often been known to spring to mind in the most unlikely circumstances.

- Sometimes writing comes to a halt because one cannot find the right word to use. It might be on the tip of the pen, but won't flow off. The best way of dealing with this kind of block rather depends on the nature of the elusive word and what you perceive to be its importance in the development of your argument or exposition. If the word is a fairly common or simple one, which, so to speak, you know you know but just can't quite dredge up from your mental dictionary, and if you can manage to carry on without it, it is often best just to leave a blank and wait for the word to come to you later. There are, however, times when the word you want is so necessary that the idea can't be quite grasped until the word is found. If, under these circumstances, you hurry on, leaving a blank or making do with a substitute, it can happen that your thought can easily begin to drift off course, even if it does not cause you to get quite lost. A major lexical block is often sufficient warning in itself that you are not as clear about what you want to say as you might have thought; so while a thesaurus may be able to help you out, you might also need to reflect more carefully on the argument of the whole paragraph or section of the essay.

1.3 Writing too much

If you are the kind of student who finds the word limits of essays an irritating restriction on your freedom to elaborate your point of view, it is well to bear in mind that there are good reasons for setting word limits. Part of the task of learning to write is to learn to select your material from the large amount of it often available and to deal with it as concisely and economically as you can. Space – whether in a journal, newspaper, book or report – is always at a premium, as is the time your readers can devote to what you write. The French polymath Pascal once apologised for having written a long letter, giving as his excuse the fact that he hadn't had the leisure to make it shorter. This is the attitude you should cultivate.

Writing too much is often the result of not having examined closely enough the RELEVANCE of what you say to the essay question or to the answer you are developing. Hence it is a good idea to begin to tackle the problem by going back to your opening to make sure that it does address the question as directly as possible. A tightly defined case in the opening leads to a more tightly argued, relevant middle. Having satisfied yourself that the opening cannot be substantially improved, scrutinise what you have written in the middle to see whether all passages contribute something substantially new to the argument – that you have not been making the same point in a number of different ways, some of which are not strictly necessary. The decision to cut such passages is often one of the hardest to make in writing, because when we are in full flight the words will flow off the pen and what looks like our finest writing will sometimes result. It is only later that we begin to realise that the flow of words has seduced us away from our main object. It is important to be ruthless in paring away any material that can be done without, no matter how well written.

Finding a balance between the amount of information we use and the depth with which we analyse it is a major subject of section 3 below.

1.4 Writing too little

Not having enough to say is perhaps a commoner problem. If you have this difficulty, the first question to ask yourself is whether you have done sufficient reading for your essay. Tutors will expect an essay to be reasonably (but not exhaustively) COMPREHENSIVE in its treatment of the topic, and this can only come from sufficiently wide reading. But there is no way in which we can say what 'sufficiently wide' will mean here in terms of the number of works you should consult. Lecturers and tutors in particular courses will sometimes give you an indication, but just as often they will not.

This is because the comprehensiveness with which you cover the available material needs to be balanced against the depth and perceptiveness with which you analyse it. An encyclopaedic store of information is of little use if you merely skate across its surface without analysing its significance to your answer. It is (as we saw in chapter 3) by developing the ability to analyse and interpret your sources in the light of your questions that you will best overcome any problem you might have in finding enough to say. In this you must learn to find your own level as early as you can, and then gradually to increase the amount of information (the number of books) your analytical skills can comfortably handle. In the rest of this chapter we shall examine the ways in which these skills are deployed in the writing of a middle.

2 The uses of outlines

Not everybody finds it useful to have a written outline of the middle to work from; some prefer to let the lines of thought develop as they write. The trouble with outlines (as we saw earlier on p. 49) is that they tend to become lists of headings that quite neglect the critical importance of establishing the relationships of logic and meaning between those headings. Even so, they can constitute a useful summary-in-advance of the ground you propose to cover, and they provide a way of provisionally allotting the number of words, paragraphs or pages you can afford to devote to any one aspect of your answer. If in writing your middle you find yourself exceeding or falling short of these limits, you are then in a position to stop and ask yourself whether the outline (in effect the essay as a whole) needs to be changed to accommodate your new emphasis or whether, on the other hand, you need to revise your approach to the section you are writing to bring it back into line with your outline. Outlines are useful not because they provide you with a fixed structure for the middle, but because they give you a provisional structure that can be changed and modified as your conception of the essay gradually matures.

3 Expanding a case

In order to justify the case put forward in the opening to your essay, it is necessary to expand on the points put forward there. This can involve you in DOING the kinds of thing we began in chapter 3 to notice other writers doing – for example defending, conceding, refuting or reconciling points of view; explaining, defining, describing or comparing various phenomena; and either generalising from evidence to an interpretation or making a generalisation stand up by recourse to particular facts, illustrations, and so on. In chapter 9 we shall be looking in more detail at how to do some of these tasks and at some of the writing problems that arise when we try to perform them successfully. In the remainder of this chapter we shall examine the most basic ways of expanding a case.

We shall do this by glancing at typical comments tutors write in the margins of essay middles and then examining how to respond to them. One of the most common – and most general – of these marginal comments is 'Needs expansion' or 'Expand on this'. What is the tutor who writes this on your essay asking you to do?

Most commonly you are being asked to do one or more of these three things:

- EXTEND your answer by considering arguments or evidence you have omitted;
- ELABORATE the point by clarifying its meaning or significance, by exemplifying it or by substantiating it with evidence;
- ENHANCE the value of a piece of information to your answer by explaining its circumstances, how or why it came to be, how it should be qualified, and so on.

You must first of all be aware that there is something of a conflict between the demands of extending your answer and those of elaborating and enhancing any part of it. This is a conflict between overall breadth of treatment and the depth with which you deal with any given point. There is no formula for reconciling these demands. One can only say that the common temptation to skate across the surface of a subject in the desire to be comprehensive should be resisted. Remember that an extensive array of information or a great variety of examples does not in itself constitute a justification of your case: you must often exclude material of marginal importance or relevance in order to make room for arguments and evidence which underpin your major points.

3.1 *Extending your answer*

Even so, the middle of an essay needs to be as comprehensive in its treatment of the subject as you can make it within the restrictions imposed by the word limit. Comprehensiveness (or breadth) comes, in the first instance, from sufficiently wide reading and, in the second, from your ability to pull the threads of your reading together. If the scope of an essay topic appears to be extremely broad (e.g. Shakespeare's tragedies, Europe of the Middle Ages, peasant societies, Western capitalism, the Third World, the symphonies of Haydn), you must read widely enough to get a general overview, while accepting the impossibility of doing justice to all this material in the body of one essay. Hence it is necessary to select just those points, cases, examples, facts, etc. sufficient to justify your case.

Typical marginal criticisms are these: 'What about. . . ?', 'Yes, but you neglect to mention . . . ' 'Not all . . . are like this', 'An alternative consideration is . . . '.

Comments such as these draw your attention to the fact that you have not read as widely as you should, or that in your reading you have either missed or ignored material the tutor considers important to your case. To guard against this kind of criticism (at least to a degree, since it is not possible always to preempt it), you can keep asking yourself these questions as you write:

- What more do I need to examine to establish this point?
  Useful linking terms: and, furthermore.
- What exceptions might there be to what I have said?
  Useful linking terms: but, except for.
- What reasonable alternatives are there to my account?
  Useful linking terms: or, alternatively, instead.

We shall examine how this works with an example. This essay topic comes from a geography course on problems of development in the Third World:

> 'Despite many well-intentioned efforts, the evidence indicates that the rural poor in many Third World countries are becoming relatively worse off.' Assess the validity of this claim.

So that we can see the case to be justified in the middle, here is a workmanlike opening to the essay. This opening wholly accedes to the proposition contained in the essay topic, arguing that it is a valid claim.

> Many attempts have been made to help the countries of the Third World out of the 'poverty trap' in which they have found themselves. The variety of techniques that have been tried, both by international aid agencies and by the governments of developing countries, has been considerable. Chief among them have been land redistribution and irrigation schemes, rural employment programmes, technological innovations and the provision of loans and credits. But the effect of all this activity has been less to help the rural poor than to give particular advantages to the richer farmers and the urban middle classes. Through their social and political influence, and through their most precious asset, capital, these groups have been able to deny to the rural poor the benefits intended by development programmes. In consequence, the gulf between the latter's living standards and those of the wealthier people in the Third World has widened dramatically.

This opening outlines the main issues to be considered in the body of the essay. It will need to be demonstrated how the aims of each of the four main types of scheme listed in the third sentence have been perverted by the intervention of influential farmers and city folk with access to capital. (Having announced that there are four main types of scheme, it is imperative for the writer not to omit consideration of any one of them. Similarly, the role of capital and of social and political influence will all have to be covered.) It will also need to be demonstrated that this intervention has actually caused a widening of the gap between rich and poor.

Here is a paragraph which takes up the issue of irrigation schemes:

> Irrigation also leads to inequality. Few Third World countries have adequate or reliable water supplies, so irrigation channels are installed. Where tanks and wells are built into the channels the larger farmers manipulate their power to obtain more water for themselves. This has been shown in Tamil Nadu in India, where pump-sets have enabled the owners of large holdings to increase their yields. They have the capital to buy and install pumps which increase their consumption of the available water, with the result that there is less water elsewhere. Poor farmers cannot afford to buy these pumps or sink deeper wells, so their share of the water diminishes steadily (Griffin and Ghose 1984: 265).

Let us now apply our three questions to this argument.

1. *What more needs to be examined?*
One example (Tamil Nadu) doesn't sufficiently constitute a case. Find and mention briefly (with reference to sources) examples of similar things happening elsewhere in developing countries.

2. *What exceptions might there be?*
The second sentence is an overgeneralisation. What about South-East Asia, parts of Latin America, etc., where water is

abundant? Are there important counterexamples to the Tamil Nadu case?

3. What alternative accounts might there be?
Owners of large holdings should not be discouraged from taking more of the water since they can put it to more efficient use. Benefits can then 'trickle down' to the rest of the community, for example in lower food prices.

By doing some more reading we can extend the argument to remedy these omissions:

> Irrigation schemes can also lead to inequality. With the exception of countries such as Korea and Taiwan, where irrigation schemes have been introduced in the wake of successful reforms in land tenure (Douglass 1983: 193–7; Griffin and Ghose 1984: 249), this is true irrespective of whether water is a scarce resource. In Indonesia the benefits of water control and irrigation schemes were not extended to smallholders because wealthier farmers would not allow their land to be crossed by small tertiary canals (Hardjono 1983: 49). The undoubted success of small irrigation schemes for the poor of Bangladesh did not stop international aid agencies putting most support into large water control schemes during the 1970s. The richer farmers profited to an extent that they could buy up the land of the poor (Hossein and Jones 1983: 164, 169–70). Development of water resources in Brazil has been directed to new large estates of over 100 hectares (Harrison 1980:69); and in Tamil Nadu, India, influential farmers with access to money for buying modern pump-sets have deprived poor peasants of much of their share of the scarce water (Griffin and Ghose 1984: 265).
>
> That disproportionate advantages should flow from irrigation to larger landholdings might be defended on the grounds of efficiency and productivity. The wealth created will 'trickle down' to the poor in the community. But in many traditional peasant economies this does not happen because the poor participate only marginally in the cash economy.

Wolf (1966: 38–9) shows how in northern India payments for goods and services are made in kind according to a system of customary rights and duties. Hence peasant farmers who produce little or no surplus for market cannot benefit from it. Savings made possible by cheaper food are restricted to those, particularly in the towns, who participate regularly in the cash economy.

3.2 Elaborating a point

Whereas extending a case involves you in searching out new material, elaboration demands that you bring out the particular implications of any general point you have already made. When we are not sure where we are going we often take refuge in vague or unsubstantiated generalisations. 'Do we know this?', 'You haven't established this', 'More elaboration needed here', 'Too general', these are the kinds of blanket comment that direct attention to the need for elaboration.

A request for elaboration forces you to clarify, substantiate or exemplify your generalisations:

- CLARIFYING a statement: make the meaning of an idea or concept more precise; or spell out a statement's significance for the point of view you are putting forward.
  Common linking terms: viz., that is to say, namely.
  Common marginal criticisms: Define this, What does this mean?, Too vague, Explain key concepts.
- SUBSTANTIATING a generalisation: refer to or quote specific evidence.
  Common linking terms: i.e., in particular, indeed.
  Common marginal criticisms: Be more precise, Demonstrate this, Give evidence, Substantiate, Be specific.
- EXEMPLIFYING a general point in such a way as to make its meaning clear and its application concrete.
  Common linking terms: e.g., for instance, inter alia.
  Common marginal criticisms: Illustrate this, Give examples.

Suppose we wanted to write a section of our middle on the

effects of the introduction of agricultural machinery on rural poverty. Our first thoughts might go something like this:

> The structure of the traditional Third World rural economy is such that the introduction of some types of agricultural machinery has led to an increase in unemployment and consequently in poverty. The wealthier have benefited from such practices because they no longer have to pay large wage bills. Instead, they can meet their costs out of savings on wages and by hiring out the machinery to other farmers who can afford to pay for it. The machinery does nothing to help the poor farmer or the landless labourer, who decline further into poverty.

There is here the germ of an argument on which we can build. What this writing lacks are those statements of clarification, substantiation and exemplification which especially characterise the middle of an academic essay.

1. What needs to be clarified?

There are two terms that need clarifying: 'the structure of the traditional Third World rural economy' and 'some types of agricultural machinery'. They need to be clarified not so much because the reader might not understand their meanings or implications but because the success of the argument which follows depends heavily on what they signify. What is it about this 'structure' which, when it is interfered with by the introduction of machinery, produces the consequences claimed? Secondly, why only 'some types' of machinery? Which types? What about those types that might not have the effects claimed?

When you find yourself using general or abstract terms like these in the first sentence or two of a paragraph, ask yourself the question 'In what does . . . consist?' Then proceed to answer it in the sentence or sentences that follow. In our example, the abstract term 'economic structure' can be thought to consist in the factors of production (land, labour, capital, etc.) and the relations between them. Different 'types of machinery' can be regarded in economic terms as capital-intensive or labour-intensive. What our writing must attempt is a clarification of each term and of how the terms are connected:

> The structure of the traditional Third World rural economy is such that the introduction of some types of machinery has led to an increase in unemployment and consequent poverty. Two characteristic features of the traditional economy are that the labour of the members of a family unit is not a 'cost of production' and that productivity is not assessed by return on capital or labour. This is because the value of labour is not thought of in terms of a wage equivalent but in terms of how much work is necessary in order to produce a subsistence living for the family (Schejtman 1984: 282). Labour is, in effect, 'unpaid'. This system need not be greatly affected by the introduction of small-scale or labour-intensive machinery. It is capital-intensive machinery which destabilises the old economic structure. This is because not only is it a cost, but unlike small-scale machinery it competes with labour. Its introduction therefore makes labour a cost.

Notice how the first part of this paragraph is structured: the general term 'economic structure' is made progressively more particular. First we are told there are two features of the structure to look at. Then we are told what those two features are. Thirdly, we are told something particular about the first of these features, labour – that it is not costed as a wage. Finally, this point is restated in everyday language.

2. What needs to be substantiated?

We have tried to clarify the effect of capital-intensive machinery on the structure of the rural economy. We have not shown, however, that it causes unemployment among the poor or that wealthier farmers prosper at their expense. This can be done by writing another paragraph, which links the evidence to the argument developed in the paragraph we wrote above:

As soon as labour becomes, thus, a cost it must compete with cost-effective mechanisation. When productivity came to be calculated on the basis of each worker as well as each acre (Hodder 1973: 138), it was accepted that tractors could often lead to savings of about one third on labour (Harrison 1979: 99). Even so, labour might not have been seriously displaced had it not been for the unfair advantage given to machinery by governments and aid agencies, which heavily subsidised the price of farm machinery when it was first introduced. In addition, they chose for pilot projects those large landholdings which could most obviously benefit from economies of scale (Griffin and Ghose 1984: 262). The effect of this was to create landless labourers where none had existed before. In Pakistan production increased less by bringing new land under cultivation than by forcing tenant farmers off previously worked land and rehiring just some of them as labourers. One study concluded that each tractor cost five jobs (Harrison 1979: 100). Similar effects have been noted with tractorisation and mechanised milling in Java (Hardjono 1983: 45, 61). Griffin and Ghose (1984: 266) quote figures which show that in Bangladesh mechanised ploughing has reduced employment by 8% to 25%, even despite its failure to produce a commensurate increase in output per acre. As with irrigation, capital-intensive mechanisation has disadvantaged the poor in all areas where it has not been accompanied by effective land reform.

In exemplifying how to clarify and substantiate the draft paragraph with which we began, we have separated these two functions into two paragraphs. This was made necessary by the fact that the first term to be clarified ('structure of the traditional Third World rural economy') is quite complex and that a sufficient amount of evidence had to be assembled to demonstrate the effect on employment of introducing machinery. When terms to be clarified are less complex (or there are few of them), you might be able to accomplish both clarification and substantiation in a single paragraph, the structure of which is fundamentally the same as that of the two paragraphs above combined. At the other extreme, you might need to take a few paragraphs just to clarify the meaning and significance of some complex terms and devote a paragraph each to the detailed examination of one piece of substantiating evidence at a time. You will see, then, that the 'shape' of a piece of writing viewed in terms of its paragraphs can contract or expand according to the demands of the content, while its basic structure is preserved intact.

You will notice in the example above that the first sentence of the first paragraph serves as a 'topic sentence' or main argument for both the paragraphs. The second sentence of the first paragraph serves as a topic sentence for that paragraph alone, while the topic of the second paragraph is found in its first sentence. It will not be difficult to imagine a situation in which a separate 'topic paragraph' might be needed to establish the main point of a whole section of the middle (rather as the opening does for the whole essay). Such variations on the basic structure of the middle must all be worked out by balancing the need for clarification and substantiation on the one hand with the word limit available to you on the other.

3 What needs to be exemplified?

Exemplifying can be performed in order to achieve some of the requirements of either clarification or substantiation. It is a characteristic of the kind of essay topic that we are dealing with here that exemplification can't easily be separated from substantiation. Hence the experience of some Third World countries which constitutes the evidence to support our argument is intended simultaneously to exemplify what one would find in the Third World as a whole. The selection of such 'examples' or 'cases' is always fraught with the danger that we are taking as typical what might on another analysis turn out not to be so typical as we had thought. (Our own examples are taken only from South and South-East Asia.) Parallel situations in other disciplines are the lines of a long poem selected for analysis, the paintings chosen from the work of a prolific artist, the particular deserts examined as examples of arid environments, the people selected as informants in a linguistic survey or an oral-history project. Except for certain statistical sampling techniques used in some social sciences, there are no sure-fire ways to ensure your examples are wholly representative. This means that you need to be on the look-out for significant exceptions – as we saw above on p. 115.

In the first of the two paragraphs above we covered ourselves by noting in the conclusion that mechanisation need not displace labour in countries with successful land reform programmes. We also restricted our argument to capital-intensive machinery, for example tractors and rice mills. You might think that we should have given examples of labour-intensive machinery in order, first, to clarify the ways in which they differ from the capital-intensive type, and secondly to substantiate the judgement that they have no significant effect on employment. This was omitted in order to save space. You will notice, however, that by choosing our words carefully ('need not be greatly affected') we tried not to make too strong a claim. A strong claim might have forced the tutor to comment 'Substantiate this'.

3.3 Enhancing the value of your information

Enhancing the value of your information requires you to qualify your main propositions by imposing certain restrictions on their truth or range of application. These restrictions are broadly concerned with time, place, manner or means, and various aspects of causation and condition. One of the problems which the draft opening paragraph of our essay (p. 114 above) poses for the middle is that it leaves little room for the development of these qualifications – it supports the proposition contained in the essay topic rather too whole-heartedly and uncritically. Some of the problems caused by this we have already had to face in writing parts of the middle. In particular we have had to make a few qualifications about place: for example, countries which have coupled development programmes with effective land reform (South Korea, Taiwan) seem to have escaped some of the worst manifestations of rural poverty.

Other problems begin to surface when we ask other questions: When? How? By what means or methods? By whom? To what degree? Why? For what reason or purpose? With what effect? Under which circumstances or conditions? In the matter of time we have been quite vague in our writing: When were these mistakes in development schemes being made? Are they still being made? There are other questions that come to mind: Who made the mistakes (central government, local officials, governments of developed countries, aid agencies, transnational corporations)? For what reasons did they attempt to solve development problems in the way they did? Do they now seem bad reasons only with the benefit of hindsight? Were the means they used inadequate to carry out their intentions? Were alternative means available? Under which conditions (social, cultural, political, economic, managerial, etc.) does it seem that some development projects fared worse than others in trying to alleviate rural poverty?

To raise questions such as these and to integrate your answers to at least some of them into the body of your essay is to make the essay more valuable in an important way. A well-qualified answer is a better answer because its propositions can be tested for their value more precisely. This means that, in the present case, if we wanted to improve programmes designed to help the rural poor we should have more variables to examine for their effect on what actually happens. For example, an irrigation scheme which has seemed to work well might work less well in another place at another time because it depends on cooperative principles which a rigidly stratified society might find very difficult to accommodate, or because local officials are venal, or because interest rates and energy costs have risen, or because the machinery is unsuitable for the terrain in which it has to work, or because of some combination of these and other conditions.

If your writing grinds to a halt or if you find that you are repeating yourself (especially in the conclusions to paragraphs), it might well be that you have not been asking yourself the kinds of question which lead to useful qualifications and which enhance the value of your information. In addition, when you have drafted a section of your middle, it is a good idea to read back over it asking these questions of the statements you have made. Often a gap can be filled just by inserting a few words (e.g. a date, a few places, a name) or a qualifying phrase which indicates the means, reason, purpose, cause, result, extent or degree. In these ways you can use the kinds of question exemplified above to help you compose, to check over what you have written and to preempt their appearing in the margin of your essay when the tutor returns it.

Let us work on the draft of a paragraph which might come towards the end of the middle:

> The failure of the many schemes and techniques discussed above led to the development of a new concept – 'integrated rural development' (IRD). Instead of focusing on just one or two needs, such as creating employment opportunities or providing loans and credits to farmers, integrated rural development studies the social, economic and physical needs of a region and tries to coordinate development on all these fronts. But even this approach has not been as successful as its advocates expected. Many of those who should have been helped have been passed by.

The first sentence raises (and does not answer) implicit questions about time and about who invented the concept IRD. The second sentence briefly clarifies the meaning of IRD but does not suggest the means by which coordination was to be achieved. The third sentence begs a very large question indeed: 'Why has IRD not been as successful as was hoped?' The last sentence betrays signs of that repetitious 'conclusion' we have seen in earlier draft paragraphs. The first thing to do is to get rid of a sentence like this, which has become stuck in the groove made by the wording of the essay topic. The next thing to do is to fill in

the gaps we have identified by inserting the necessary qualifications:

> As early as 1959 it had become clear to those who set up the
> Comilla project in what was then East Pakistan that piecemeal
> introduction of the schemes and techniques discussed above
> was not working (Harrison 1980: 83). Fertilizer and new seed
> were of little use to a farmer who had no access to credit, little
> knowledge of how to use these innovations or little incentive
> to risk new techniques alone. The Comilla project organised
> cooperatives and coordinated government assistance,
> education, public health, the provision of credit, the
> introduction of new farming techniques and so on. This
> approach later came to be known as 'integrated rural
> development' (IRD), which tries to take all the relevant social,
> economic and physical factors into account and to integrate
> their introduction into a designated locality. Particular
> emphasis is placed on the participation of all the people and on
> finding local solutions consistent both with traditional
> customs and national development priorities (Lea and
> Chaudhri 1983: 13).

Lea and Chaudhri acknowledge that there have been some
success stories and they list the ingredients for success
(p. 17). But too often these projects have not lived up to
expectations because, as Harrison (1980: 84) puts it,
'integrated rural development . . . is not integrated enough':
there are just too many factors which interact in ways we do
not sufficiently understand. Moreover, the wishes and needs
of the local people can be quite incompatible with the
economic and political priorities of central government. A
number of local or regional successes might have no
discernible impact on national programmes, while national
successes can seriously harm local and regional projects (Lea
and Chaudhri 1983: 18). Quick and clear success stories in
rural development should not therefore be expected in
circumstances that cannot be fully controlled, owing, for
instance, to the state of our knowledge or the processes of
competing political or economic interests. If IRD has shown

nothing else, it is now clear that there is no simple technical 'fix' to the problems of rural poverty.

In this expansion of the draft paragraph the 'when', 'where', 'by whom' and 'how' questions are dispatched in the first paragraph. The large 'Why has IRD not succeeded?' question is given a paragraph to itself, a paragraph which opens by CON-CEDING that there have been some successes. The paragraph suggests two reasons for the failure of IRD and concludes, in effect, that it is not particularly helpful to blame anyone for its failures.

Having worked my way through the material and come to this conclusion about IRD, I find that the essay opening with which we began (p. 114 above) needs a few changes to make it consonant with what I now think to be a more mature conception of the problem. It is not so much a change of answer that is needed as a change in emphasis. It is true that the measures listed in the opening have not solved the problems of the rural poor, and it remains true that the better-off have benefited most. But even the best and most recent endeavours to change all this are often compromised by rather deep-seated issues that do not admit of easy solutions. The adjustments to the opening should indicate the substance of this major qualification.

Certain changes of emphasis in parts of the middle are also called for. Does the failure of irrigation schemes now deserve all the space given to it? Perhaps what is said about irrigation can be generalised to include other technological innovations and integrated with the section on machinery. Secondly, should not more space be given to analysing development initiatives that have had some success in helping the rural poor? The aim of this section would be to identify those factors which distinguish these initiatives. Useful comparisons between successful and unsuccessful schemes could then be drawn.

Expansion necessarily involves writing at greater length than we did in our first drafts on any particular issue. What this compels is a reassessment of the space and prominence given to any one of those issues if we are to keep within the word limit. In coping with the requirements of extending, elaborating and enhancing our main points or propositions we are faced simultaneously with having to reduce the number of issues we can cover adequately. This can be done, as suggested above, by combining a few relatively particular topics like 'irrigation' and 'machinery' into a more general one such as 'technological innovations', and by choosing one or two of the particulars to examine in some detail as examples or case studies. Striking a balance between extending an answer and elaborating and enhancing the parts of it is one of the arts of writing. In creating any work of art we cannot make final judgements about the parts until we have developed some sense of the whole. This is why everything in your middle (as well as your opening) must be regarded as a provisional draft until you have finished this part of the essay.

3.4 A note on the use of sources

The sources used above are the following:

Harrison, P. (1979) *Inside the Third World*. Harmondsworth, Middlesex: Penguin

Harrison, P. (1980) *The Third World Tomorrow*. Harmondsworth, Middlesex: Penguin

Hodder, B. W. (1973) *Economic Development in the Tropics*, 2nd edn. London: Methuen

Lea, D. A. M. and Chaudhri, D. P. (eds.) (1983) *Rural Development and the State*. London and New York: Methuen.

Wilber, C. K. (ed.) (1984) *The Political Economy of Development and Underdevelopment*, 3rd edn. New York: Random House

Wolf, E. (1966) *Peasants*. Englewood Cliffs, New Jersey: Prentice-Hall

The references in the passages above to Douglass, to Hardjono and to Hossein and Jones are all to papers in the book edited by Lea and Chaudhri. The references to Griffin and Ghose and to Schejtman are to papers in the Wilber book of readings.

You will see that I have relied heavily on just a few books. It is this reliance which has produced the rather one-dimensional answer we began to have doubts about in rewriting the last of the sections above. Hence, in order to EXTEND our answer to take account of the new emphasis, and to substantiate that extension, it would be necessary to read more widely. Even so, if you compare the use of sources in our very first draft paragraphs with that in our expansions, you will see that one can extract a great deal more from the references immediately at hand than might at first seem possible. The poet and critic T. S. Eliot once observed that Shakespeare had learned far more about history from the single volume of *Plutarch's Lives* than most people could from the whole history collection of the British Museum library. The ability to ELABORATE and ENHANCE your points by writing in some depth depends not just on reading more widely in the search for facts but also on reading the sources at hand in more depth.

4 Summary

Drafting the middle of the essay is a test of a number of things:

- First it is a test of how well you have drafted your opening and of the usefulness of any outline of issues to be covered you have made.
- Secondly, it is a test of your ability to conceptualise the material in such a way that breadth of coverage is balanced against the need to elaborate and enhance.
- Thirdly, it is a test of how well you are able to use the common experience of grinding to a halt to rethink where a line of argument is taking you or to ask new and relevant questions about how to enhance the points you have already made.
- Finally, it is a test of your willingness not to be wholly imprisoned by the draft of your opening or by the draft of any part of the middle, and of your readiness to change the emphasis in your answer. Only rarely should you feel the need to change the fundamental thrust of your answer and to

rewrite from the beginning. If this does happen, remember that the new assurance with which you write will compensate magnificently for the extra labour.

All these tests are ones you should try to set for yourself. The comments of other students and your tutors are (or can be) invaluable aids in helping you to recognise where something needs to be extended, elaborated or enhanced. But writing and rewriting the middle remains most importantly the opportunity to test out for yourself the argument of the draft opening with which you began.

6
Endings

[In the Epilogue] you must make the
audience well-disposed towards
yourself . . .

ARISTOTLE

1 Recapitulation

If we present our conclusions at the beginning of the essay, how
do we 'conclude' it?

There is an element of truth in the old preacher's advice to a
young cleric beginning on a career of writing sermons: 'First you
tell them what you're going to tell them, then you tell them, and
last you tell them what you told them.' RECAPITULATING your
arguments and emphasising the most important aspects of them
is just one function of an ending and will not be recommended in
all disciplines or in all departments. Such recapitulation should
aim, as Aristotle advises, to refresh your readers' memories and
make your points 'easily understood'. By choosing the words in
which you express your recapitulation with care, you can simultaneously indicate which of the issues you have raised or arguments you have used are the most important. In any recapitulation there will inevitably be a degree of repetition, even of
some of the very words and phrases used in the opening or
middle. But the ending should nevertheless avoid being simply a
rewriting – a mere repetition – of the opening.

Now, there are various ways in which this can be achieved.
First of all, it is important to be aware that recapitulation is itself
not a *necessary* constituent of an ending at all. There is no
uniformly observed rule (Aristotle or the old preacher notwith-

standing) which says the ending must contain a systematic review. If you are confident that your exposition in the opening and the middle has been clear, you may prefer to end on a note of paradox, aphorism, larger generalisation or particular concrete instance which sums up the issues you have been discussing in an oblique manner. Essays in literature and the fine arts often end this way. Indeed, unlike openings (various styles of which we recommended in chapter 4), endings have no really necessary constituents at all. Recapitulation and the other features of endings discussed below are all optional. All we can say with any confidence is that your essay must have some kind of ending which is distinguishable from the middle. It is the ending that provides a sense of 'closure' and unity to the composition as a whole.

Another general point to bear in mind is that, though styles of endings are optional, the choice may not be wholly free. Some disciplines may tend to favour or frown upon certain kinds of ending. Some kinds of essay topic or subject matter may prompt the choice of one kind of ending over another. For example, in those disciplines or subjects of the social sciences which lend themselves to experimental, survey or participant research, it is frequently proper to conclude by summing up the present state of knowledge and to suggest what further research needs to be done. This may be out of place in an essay which focuses on the interpretation of somebody's writings – say a novelist, a political scientist or a theoretical sociologist. I have made no attempt in what follows to give you systematic advice about the appropriateness of varying endings to different disciplines, subject matters or types of essay topic. You will be able to pick up hints about this by looking at conclusions in the secondary sources you read for your essays. What I shall do here is to point out some of the things to look for.

2 Mood: suggestion and implication

Where you do use your ending to recapitulate your main points or arguments, it can be saved from being a mere repetition –

slightly reworded – of the opening by a change in your mood. One of the opportunities an ending provides to the writer is the chance to reflect upon what he has written. The dominant mood of an opening is stating or asserting. That of the middle is justifying. Both need to be vigorous and closely focused on the essay topic itself. Your ending, by contrast, can afford to relax a little, even sometimes to go so far as to admit that your argument has not solved all the problems raised by the question. The focus may shift from the topic itself to your own discussion of the topic.

One of the words often found in the conclusions to academic papers is 'suggest'. For example 'I have tried to suggest that the distinction commonly drawn between "social democracy" and "democratic socialism" tends to distract our attention from the very fundamental characteristics they have in common.' In thus summing up a major concern of the essay the writer has adopted a new mood to his thesis. There is here a certain modesty or tentativeness about what the essay has achieved – a recognition that one is contributing to a process of learning and discussion larger than oneself. This, broadly speaking, is a helpful attitude to adopt (even, perhaps, when your essay has been a vigorous refutation of some opponent's views) for, having thus put yourself in this mood, you might be led to cast your eye afresh over your own arguments or over their overall importance in your field of study.

Students often lack confidence in their arguments anyway, so 'suggesting' might come quite naturally. But there is a danger here, a danger just as present even to experienced academic writers. This is that modest SUGGESTION can become ritualised or formulaic and so lose the kind of sincerity that may be necessary to its success. A fault to be found sometimes in the closing paragraphs of papers in academic journals is a degree of diffidence so great that the reader may come to doubt the seriousness of the whole piece of work. W. G. Runciman, an eminent sociologist who has written lots of very good things, begins the conclusion to one of his essays thus:

> This rapid and rather cavalier survey of a complex topic cannot
> suggest more than a very tentative general conclusion. But if
> my argument is at all well founded, it suggests that . . .

The back-pedalling here is so furious, overgeneralised and drawn
out that I begin to suspect either a false modesty or that the
author himself suspects his argument cannot withstand much
serious scrutiny.

One way of tackling this problem in your own writing is to
make an attempt to separate those aspects of your thesis or
argument about which you feel quite confident from those
which are rather more tentative. Your conclusion can then draw
attention to this distinction in a purposeful way. Something of
this comes through in the extract below. The authors might not
be doing justice to themselves, and in summing up their paper
they could have expressed the distinction between solid gain and
tentative suggestion more clearly. It is, however, genuine. This
conclusion comes from a paper in linguistics by R. N. Campbell
and R. J. Wales which has argued that the way in which gram-
marians have treated comparison (or comparative structures)
has been too superficial to explain issues of meaning and logic:

> Clearly, much of what we have suggested is speculative. In
> particular, our grammatical suggestions require extensive
> justification which it is not possible to provide here. It may
> therefore turn out that some or all of our proposals are
> ill-founded. Our main purpose has been to re-open discussion
> of comparative structures with a view to revising the older type
> of analysis, which we believe to have been unsatisfactory in
> that it assigned superficial status to the linguistic expression of
> what we believe to be a fundamental linguistic, logical and
> intellectual operation.

In effect, the authors are saying, we cannot be sure that we have
got the details of the grammar right, but we are sure, nevertheless, that the general approach to analysis we have taken is the
most fruitful one.

You will see from this extract that the authors have done

something else besides suggesting and recapitulating. In the second and third sentences they have also raised the matter of the relation between their paper and the further study of this topic: their own grammatical proposals require 'extensive justification'. This is an example of another characteristic feature of conclusions, a feature I am inclined to think is the most important.

This is that a conclusion will often look at the IMPLICATIONS of the work carried out in the essay. 'Implication', like 'suggest', is a commonly recurring word in conclusions to academic papers. Implications can be expressed in a variety of ways, some being particularly favoured in certain disciplines. When we ask ourselves a question about implications, we must add the corollary 'Implications for what?'. Here are some of the favourite answers in academic writing:

- the implications for the further study of the subject (PROPOSING);
- the implications for our assessment of present or past approaches to the subject (REVALUING);
- the implications of my narrowly focused, empirical work for more general, more theoretical, or different but related issues (GENERALISING, EXTRAPOLATING);
- the implications of my general or more theoretical work for the illumination of particular, empirical questions (CONTEXTUALISING);
- the implications of my analysis for solutions to practical or applied problems (RECOMMENDING, APPLYING);
- the implications of my analysis of some present or contemporary issue for the prediction of what might happen in the future (PREDICTING);
- the implications of my analysis of some past event or situation for the better understanding of some later event outside the immediate focus of the essay topic (ANTICIPATING).

All of these require the writer to stand back from the immediate details of his answer: to look backwards, forwards, or more generally around him, and to establish a context in which his answer can be placed.

An indication of the implications of your work may also be thought of as an evaluation of its *significance*. Any such evaluation is subject to dangers similar to the ones surrounding 'suggesting'. In this case, by contrast, the danger seems to lie in overvaluing the implications or significance of your work. Not a few academic papers conclude with rather large claims which may be little more than thinly veiled appeals for research funds or for other researchers to jump on the bandwagon. It will often be betrayed by either a fuzziness or a very strident tone in the language. Notice, for example, the 'musts' and the 'should' in the extract below. It is the conclusion to an article in the journal *Language in Society* on how pupils' manners of speech can unfairly influence their teachers' assessment of their ability. (You will also see in this conclusion various of the kinds of implication from the list above):

> We suggest that teachers must be made more aware of the process by which they evaluate their students. It is the responsibility of the teaching colleges to impress on aspiring teachers that their decisions about students must be made cautiously, and always with regard to their educational implications.
>
> The results of the present study, however, have only begun to illuminate the dynamics of the student–teacher interaction. The direction for future research is evident. In addition to taking into account the intrinsically active nature of interpersonal relationships by varying the stimulus modality and using video-taped stimulus materials, other studies should be conducted systematically varying the social class, ethnic background, role, sex and age of both speakers and judges. These investigations must examine the importance of speech characteristics relative to other personal attributes while at the same time investigating the *relative* importance or contribution of various speech characteristics to the complex task of person perception.

No reasonable person, I suppose, would quarrel too seriously with the generalised suggestions of the first paragraph in this conclusion (though the 'suggest' seems ritualistic in such close company with 'must'). What is more alarming is the implication in the second paragraph that nobody much has thought about this matter before, and that anybody who wants to 'should' and 'must' follow the research programme founded and prescribed by these researchers. This reveals ignorance and arrogance, as does the implication that the use of the fuzzy, jargonesque 'complex task of person perception' makes new and different what good teachers since Socrates have always attempted – understanding and judging students fairly. These authors lack perspective on their subject.

This example is therefore cautionary. Most readers of this book will be students who may not have had the chance to develop a broader perspective on their work. Discussing its implications will therefore be quite difficult. It is not, however, impossible if you keep two things in mind (and these two things apply equally to the handling of 'suggestions'). First, avoid the very large and general claim (e.g. 'illuminating the dynamics of the student–teacher interaction') and concentrate on the particular issues raised in your essay as a starting point. Secondly, do not ignore the needs of a conclusion until you find them staring you in the face. If putting forward implications is important, then you must be looking out for these wider significances when you are doing your reading and note-taking. A well-written and carefully thought-out conclusion will fulfil another of Aristotle's prescriptions for an epilogue: 'make the audience well-disposed towards yourself . . .'.

3 Variations on a theme

We conclude with a few examples of ways in which one essay might be brought to an end. On the optional constituents discussed above – recapitulating, suggesting, and discussing implications – we shall conduct a few variations.

So that you can see what is being varied a trifle more clearly, I shall first present the opening of the essay. (Considerations of space preclude the presentation of the middle.) The opening was written by a first-year undergraduate, and isn't bad. It presents the main issues discussed in the body of the essay clearly and directly. The different endings (which I have concocted) refer back to this opening, and also to some of the major points the student raises in the body of her essay. The topic is: 'Discuss the principal reasons for the evolution of detente in American–Soviet relations.'

Opening

A fear of total nuclear war, combined with an understanding of the balance of terror, was the overwhelming reason for the evolution of detente between the United States and the Soviet Union. Shifts in the American perception of the nature of communism and of its own role in the world created a greater sense of trust between the states, while the realisation of national needs made this new relationship imperative to both superpowers.

Our first conclusion gives considerable space to a fairly detailed RECAPITULATION. It then goes on to widen the interpretation of detente in terms of the balance of terror and the balance of power and the 'symbiosis' (a rather old-fashioned metaphor) that grew up between the superpowers. It finishes (as do the others) by raising an issue which, though outside the strict terms of the essay topic, places detente in its immediate context: the fact that it failed SUGGESTS that something was wrong with the reasons behind it.

Conclusion 1

I have suggested that the main reasons for detente were concern for security and the need to further mutual interests, particularly in the economic, industrial and technological spheres. We have seen how the balance of terror made it clear that a first-strike capability was not enough, and how the Hungarian uprising and the Cuban missile crisis produced an understanding between the superpowers about 'spheres of influence'. We have also seen how events in the Middle East,

Vietnam and elsewhere did not fundamentally disturb this arrangement, but how the emergence of China complicated the geopolitical map of the world, in such a way that neither the USA nor the USSR could predict her response in a crisis. All these issues conspired to produce a certain identity of interest between the superpowers, an identity that was cemented by the SALT talks and the trade agreements of 1972.

The fact is that by the 1970s the two main antagonists had come to depend upon one another to maintain a balance not only of terror but of power, too. It was a classic case of political symbiosis. The balance of power might not have been disturbed even by the Soviet entry into Afghanistan if the USA had not upset the balance of terror by the development of 'theatre' nuclear weapons and talk of winning a limited nuclear war. Under these circumstances 'national interest' could not carry the burden of detente alone.

Our second conclusion restricts the recapitulation to little other than a restatement of the opening sentence of the essay. It then goes on to question the answer given and to PREDICT the success of any future attempts at detente.

Conclusion 2

In suggesting that the fundamental reasons behind detente were concern for domestic security and the desire to satisfy individual national interests we have nevertheless begged one important question. The need for domestic security and the requirements of national interest have not diminished since the early 1970s. Why, then, has detente collapsed? It may be that both the USA and the USSR perceived the objectives we have discussed to be sufficient in themselves. What they did not address seriously was a more fundamental issue – coexistence between communist and capitalist ideologies. Until it is addressed future attempts at detente can hardly hope to be more successful. The motivations behind detente in the 1960s and early 1970s paradoxically contained the cause of its later demise.

Our third looks at a different set of IMPLICATIONS. The adequacy of the answer given is questioned and a possible reinterpretation suggested. The latter's adequacy is set aside for lack of evidence, but a future development in the study of the reasons for detente is PROPOSED.

Conclusion 3

There seems to be a broad consensus among commentators on those reasons for detente we have identified – primarily the concern for domestic security and the desire to satisfy national economic and technological interests. But, while these reasons sufficiently explain detente, what this consensus leaves room for doubt about is whether they were the real reasons for both the USA and the USSR. The USSR's adventure in Afghanistan is evidence for some Western observers that she had merely been using detente as a mask for traditional communist expansionism, and that the USA had been duped by detente. Whether this is in fact the case cannot be decided on the evidence available. The implications for the understanding of detente are nevertheless important. For if the USA was pursuing security and national interest as ends in themselves while the USSR was using the same objectives only as a means to something else, then the interpretation of many of the events that led to detente will need to be revised.

Using the information you will have gleaned from the paragraphs above, you could try, if you wish, to write another ending to this essay.

Part III

Language

7
You, your language and your material

How can we know the dancer from the dance?

One of the main themes in this book has been that an essay is *your* best answer to a question. If the essay is to be *your* answer, rather than *the* answer or *an* answer or *someone else's* answer, it is necessary to start paying close attention to some of the problems that arise in your use of language as you strive to establish a relationship with the material you have to mould. In this chapter we shall study a few of these problems. The first is an old bugbear – whether one should use 'I' in an academic essay. But there are others which can just as easily arise if you are uncertain about your position as a scholar and writer – if you tend to assume or try to pretend that you have no significant part to play in putting a construction on the material you find in your sources.

1 Subjective and objective: the uses of 'I' and 'we'

There is much confusion, not just in students' minds but in tutors' too, on whether 'I' and 'we' may be used in academic writing. Some tutors encourage you to be direct in your writing and to use 'I'. Others perpetuate an old myth that if you use 'I' your writing is too 'subjective'. You will probably find that the two words 'subjective' and 'objective' are very commonly flung about in your university or college as a shorthand to distinguish the unreliable and idiosyncratic opinions of individuals from the tried and tested truths of science or scholarship.

Preferences are obvious examples of subjectivity. For example, 'I like Picasso prints in my bathroom' states no more than an individual idiosyncrasy. A statement like this is often confused with ones that can look rather similar: 'I think Machiavelli's reputation as an amoral rogue is thoroughly undeserved'; or 'I conclude that D. H. Lawrence wrote only two really good novels, neither of which is *Sons and Lovers*'. Now, whether or not these two statements are subjective has absolutely nothing to do with the use of 'I'. It depends entirely on whether these judgements have been justified (or are to be justified) in the piece of language of which they form the conclusion. You can see that the presence or absence of justification is not affected if you take out the introductory phrases 'I think . . . ' and 'I conclude that . . . '. Judgements, as we have seen, should be personal. Whether or not they are also objective depends on argument and evidence, not on whether you introduce them with an 'I'. Similarly, a purely subjective opinion or preference is not made objective by changing 'I' to 'we'.

The fact that 'I' can be, and is, used in academic writing is not to say, nevertheless, that every judgement you make should be flagged by 'I think', 'I believe', 'it seems to me' or some equivalent expression. The reason for this should by now be quite straightforward. This is that, since your essay should by definition be an account of your own justified judgements and beliefs, nothing is to be gained by continually making this explicit. 'I' is best used sparingly and reserved for a few typical situations:

1 When you need to make it clear to the reader that a judgement is your own and not to be confused with that of an author whose judgements you have been reporting or discussing; or when you want to emphasise where you stand with respect to other work, for example whether you want to agree, concede, rebut, question, reformulate, reconcile, etc. (see chapter 3, section 4):

Unlike Leavis, I believe the structure of *Sons and Lovers* seriously flawed.

> While conceding to most critics that the Ninth Symphony is a work of grandeur, I question whether Beethoven avoided parodying himself.

2 When you wish to emphasise your own degree of confidence in the outcome of your reasoning:

> Given the unreliability of some of this evidence I think it impossible to draw any firm conclusion.

> This [evidence] suggests to me that Michelangelo was just as concerned to preserve his reputation for being different from other architects as to correct any supposed shortcomings in Bramante's design for St Peter's.

3 When you want to announce to your reader how you propose to proceed or what modes of analysis you are engaging in:

> I shall try to demonstrate that . . .

> I have defined poverty in relative terms.

> Before describing what happened, I shall explain the background to these events.

'We' has two common uses, neither of which, as we saw above, should be to pretend that a personal judgement is a generally accepted 'objective' judgement. The legitimate uses of 'we' are these:

1 When you wish to report a conclusion that your reading has actually shown you to be generally accepted. 'We' in this usage includes 'I' the writer, 'you' the reader and 'them', other scholars (i.e. it means 'we all'). The verbs most commonly used with 'we' in this way are 'know' and 'believe':

> We know that as early as 1942 the Allies had plenty of information on what was happening to Jews in the concentration camps.

> We believe that the short-term memory capacity of the brain is 7 ± 2 units or 'chunks' of information.

2 When you the writer wish to guide the reader through what you propose to do or what you have already done in your essay. In this usage 'we' includes 'I' and 'you' (the reader) but excludes others. It is most frequently used with verbs of observation, perception and analysis (e.g. see, observe, inspect, analyse, examine, find):

> When we come to examine whether the Allies deliberately ignored the plight of the Jews, we shall find the evidence is not conclusive.

> When we analyse the second stanza of the poem, we discover that the rhyme scheme has become even more complex.

> We have seen in *Heart of Darkness* how Marlow's narrative distorts the sequence of the events as they must actually have happened to him. Now we must ask what structural implications Conrad's experimenting with time has for this novel.

3 When an essay or article is written by more than one author, in which case 'we' will be employed for those uses of 'I' set out above. Since most, if not all, of your essays will be written alone, you should have little need for this use of 'we'.

Acquiring confidence in your use of 'I' and 'we' should help you to define more clearly for yourself your relationship with the material, with other scholars' judgements on it and with your reader. It should, in addition, help you to avoid some of the pitfalls in structuring sentences and clarifying meanings that await those who try to write in a spuriously objective style. To these pitfalls we now turn.

2 Confusing yourself with your material

2.1 Dangling modifiers

It might seem quite improbable that you would confuse yourself with what you are writing about. But people often structure their sentences in such a way that this seems to be happening. Let us rewrite a few of the examples above using structures that are quite common:

When examining whether the Allies deliberately ignored the plight of the Jews the evidence is not conclusive.

Unlike Leavis, the structure of *Sons and Lovers* is seriously flawed.

Before describing what happened, the background to these events must be understood.

Examining the second stanza of the poem, the rhyme scheme is even more complex.

These sentences exemplify what are sometimes called 'dangling modifiers'. The first part of each sentence is said to 'modify' the main proposition, which is contained in the second part of the sentence. These modifying phrases 'dangle' because, as you will see, the nature of the subject has changed in the transition from the modifying phrase to the main proposition. In each of the cases above this has been caused by the writer's failure to distinguish between what he or she does (examine, judge, describe) and what is being talked about (evidence, Leavis, background, rhyme scheme). Put another way, the structure of these sentences makes it appear that the evidence is doing the examining, the structure of *Sons and Lovers* is unlike Leavis, the background is describing what happened and the rhyme scheme is examining the poem. While you will recognise these to be absurdities, you might be tempted to say that what is intended is quite clear. In fact, it isn't always clear what the writer intended and, in any case, we should always strive not only to mean what we say but also to say what we mean.

The third example illustrates these problems quite well, for there is a double slip here which has been caused by the writer not having clarified the distinction between self and material. The use of the verb 'understand' (in place of the 'explain' used in the earlier version of this sentence on p. 145 above) implies that the writer must be doing the understanding as well as the describing. Actually, the writer probably means that it is the reader and writer together who must understand the background to the events ('understand' is a verb which, in academic writing, is more typically found with 'we' than 'I' as its subject). This sentence has muddled up writer, reader and object of enquiry.

As soon as you begin to use the language of enquiry (in these cases verbs like 'examine', 'describe' and 'understand'), take care that you use 'I' or 'we' appropriately. The other recourse is to make no reference at all to what you do, for example:

> The evidence that the Allies deliberately ignored the plight of the Jews is not conclusive.

> The rhyme scheme of the second stanza is even more complex.

But to eschew wholly the language of enquiry is to make impossible such statements of disagreement and analytical intention as the second and third examples above try to do. Hence it is necessary to learn to feel comfortable about using such language. As you practise such usages in your writing, scrutinise them carefully to ensure that you have not confused the processes that properly belong to the writer (I), to the writer and reader (we), and to the matter being written about.

2.2 Passives

Similar care is needed when you use the passive voice of a verb instead of the active voice. In the active voice the person or phenomenon performing the action is made quite explicit:

> I have defined poverty in relative terms.

> When we examine whether the Allies deliberately ignored the plight of the Jews, we find the evidence to be inconclusive.

In these sentences 'I' and 'we' are performing the respective actions of defining and examining, the active voice making this quite clear. If, on the other hand, we write these sentences in the passive voice, the subjects disappear and a vagueness of meaning can creep in:

Poverty has been defined in relative terms.

When the evidence that the Allies deliberately ignored the plight of the Jews is examined, it is found to be inconclusive.

In these sentences the questions begged are '*Who* has defined poverty in this way?' and '*Who* examined the evidence and thinks it inconclusive?'. It is no longer quite clear whether the writer is simply reporting what other scholars have done or whether the writer is affirming his or her own judgement. Your tutor will probably assume the first of these interpretations, and will immediately demand that you EXPAND on these statements by giving references to sources, and by suggesting that there are alternative definitions of poverty you have ignored or that not all scholars think the evidence inconclusive (see chapter 5).

Using the active voice forces you to decide quite definitely whether you are giving your own judgement, reporting that of just some scholars or reporting what is a generally accepted judgement. However, if it *is* your own judgement that is being made here, the passive voice can be kept just so long as you make this position clear in some other way. A reference to your own essay text is one such way:

Poverty has been defined *above* in relative terms.

When the evidence that the Allies deliberately ignored the plight of the Jews *comes to be* examined *below*, it will be shown to be inconclusive.

These statements are now announcements to the reader about what you have done or what you will do in your text, a function of language very different from the delivering of a judgement. They will not therefore attract a request to EXPAND.

Some books on writing counsel their readers always to avoid the passive voice. This is ridiculous. What you must do when you use the passive is to ensure that you have not begged a significant question about the identity of the actor. This is particularly important when the distinction between what you are saying and what others have said is at stake.

2.3 Time and tense

A third source of confusion between oneself and one's material is the failure to realise that, very often, we as writers and scholars may inhabit a slightly different universe of time from some of the things we write about. Consequently, there are certain conventions about the use of tenses – especially past and present – in academic writing which are not intuitively obvious. You will probably be quite familiar with the straightforward convention which decrees that events which happened in the past are written about in the past tense. (So in history essays we will write that 'Napoleon *retreated* from Moscow in disarray' rather than adopt the style of some television documentaries. In the latter, narrators – in the manner of sports commentators – will tell us 'Napoleon *retreats* from Moscow in disarray' as we watch some painting or re-enactment of this event.) But problems begin to arise when we draw distinctions between reporting or describing past events on the one hand (what Napoleon did) and interpreting them on the other (what I believe or argue Napoleon did). They also arise when we are dealing with certain kinds of material – in particular, texts written in the past or societies studied by anthropologists at some time in the past.

Look at the use of tenses in this extract from George H. Sabine's *A History of Political Theory*. In his passage Sabine is discussing the view of the eighteenth-century English statesman Edmund Burke that the rights of man are founded not so much in nature as in the conventions established by a civilised society:

> It is true that [Burke] never denied the reality of natural rights.
> Like Hume he admitted that the social contract may be true
> merely as a bit of hypothetical history, and much more than
> Hume he was convinced that some of the conventions of
> society are inviolable. Just what these immovable principles are
> he never tried to say – property, religion, and the main outlines
> of the political constitution would probably have been among
> them – but he certainly believed in their reality. However,
> again like Hume, he believed that they were purely

conventional. That is to say, they arise not from anything belonging to nature or to the human species at large, but solely from the habitual and prescriptive arrangements that make a body of men into a civil society.

Sabine uses the past tense to report *that* Burke did or believed certain things (e.g. 'denied', 'admitted', 'was convinced', 'tried', 'believed'). These are treated as (past) events in Burke's mental life. But when Sabine wishes to emphasise either his own point of view ('it is true') or the ideas themselves, which are just as present to Sabine as he writes as they were to Burke and his contemporaries when Burke wrote about them, he shifts to what is called the 'universal' present tense. (Sabine slips up once: 'he believed they *were* purely conventional'.) The activity of Burke's thinking is a past event in history; what he thought about is still 'present' to the modern reader in Burke's texts.

Hence it is usual to use the present tense to write about what you find in texts no matter when they were written. If you are a literature student, in particular, you need to remember this convention, since most of your writing is about what is found in texts. You might write that Milton *believed* so and so, but that in *Paradise Lost* he *says* such and such.

There is a problem with yet another dimension of time that you must keep in mind as you write about literature. This is that you should not confuse the time dimension in which you operate while you read a work with the space–time sequence of words on the printed page. That is to say, you should avoid making statements like this:

> When reading the poem, as we noticed the mood change between lines 6 and 8 so did the diction.

This use of tenses suggests that the diction of the poem changed as we were reading the poem and noticed the mood changing. What has been confused here is a report about 'our' reading processes (a psychological and historical event) and a report about what is on the printed page (a literary phenomenon). The diction, like the mood, changes between lines 6 and 8, not between the time we began to read line 6 and the time we finished line 8. In general, it is probably better to omit any reference to the private activity of reading a text (whatever your discipline) and to concentrate, rather, on the conclusions your reading has brought you to. In this way you will more readily be led to justify these conclusions by pointing to the evidence in the text instead of dressing up your own reading activities as 'our' objective literary experiences: the 'we' in the sentence above should really be 'I'.

If you are a student of sociology, anthropology, or another social science which requires the reporting of field-work in which you have engaged, you must make a slightly different distinction in the use of tenses. When you are reporting particular events you observed, interviews you conducted or other such observational activities of your own, the past tense is appropriate. But the moment you begin to generalise about these observations, to describe the behaviour of groups or institutions, you should move into what is called the 'ethnographic present tense', a conventional tense which locates the writer and the subject matter in the same time frame. Even if you have good cause to believe that, as you write, aspects of the social structure you are writing about have changed significantly (not uncommon in anthropology), you will maintain the present tense.

Notice how in this extract about the Nuer in southern Sudan, E. E. Evans-Pritchard (in A. R. Radcliffe-Brown and D. Forde (eds.), *African Systems of Kinship and Marriage*) moves from the present tense, in which he makes general statements or interpretations, to the past tense, in which he reports a particular experience of his own which illustrates his general point:

> Nevertheless, in spite of their many contacts with one another and of their concerted action in their relations with other villages, there may be rivalries between different parts of a single village ... *Wa pekda*, 'I go to my end (of the village)', often indicates, besides direction, a particular loyalty within

the wider village. As an example of this feeling I mention an experience in the village of Nyueny, which is referred to again later. I gave spears to two youths who often visited me from the other end of the village than that where I had pitched my tent, and a man at our end protested to me in private...

Much of the research on which Evans-Pritchard bases his essay is now forty or fifty years old, and it is very likely that certain aspects of Nuer social organisation have changed in that time. Even so, if you were to be using this essay as a source for one of your own essays, the convention is that you use the present tense for generalisations about the Nuer just as Evans-Pritchard has done in his first three sentences. Only if you had access to more recent research which shows that changes have taken place, and only if you were writing about social change, would you use the past tense where he has used the present. In this way you can use tense to help define your own position with respect to changes in knowledge or in the society being studied.

Switching between present and past tenses (even within the same sentence) is common in academic writing – as the Sabine extract above illustrates. What is important is that you make these switches in a principled way, for example to signal a shift between your own interpretations and your reports of events, and that you be consistent. Checking consistency in your use of tense is one of the jobs that must be carried out when revising your drafts.

2.4 Your own text and others' texts

Another confusion that can easily arise is one between what you write and what the authors of your sources have written. You need to manipulate your language with some care when you are writing about the sources you are using if you are to avoid running together what is in those texts with what is in your own, or (to put it another way) to avoid running together what the authors of the sources do with what you do.

Note, first, that a quotation is most often something that you

performed. A quotation is not something written by the
rce you are using. Hence, rather than write,

> This quotation *by* Evans-Pritchard shows that loyalty among
> the Nuer does not extend to the whole village,

you should write,

> This quotation *from* Evans-Pritchard shows that . . .

The difference between 'by' and 'from' distinguishes between
who is responsible for the action (of quoting) and the person
affected by the action. You (the writer) are the person who is
actually quoting, whereas Evans-Pritchard is merely being used
by you as a source material you are drawing *from*. If you find
yourself vacillating between 'by' and 'from' as you write, try to
sort out the position in terms such as these.

Here is a similar problem:

> The Commission's activity broadened to encompass other
> aspects of urban renewal, as outlined by Coleman (1970) in
> section 3.1 above.

The best way to get this to say what, apparently, was intended is
to make it quite explicit who wrote section 3.1 above by using 'I'
or 'we' and also to make it clear who is doing the outlining – I
(the writer) or Coleman. For example:

> In section 3.1 above I outlined Coleman's (1970) account of
> how the Commission's activity broadened to encompass other
> aspects of urban renewal.

or:

> In section 3.1 above we examined Coleman's (1970) outline of
> how the Commission's activity broadened to encompass other
> aspects of urban renewal.

Finally, take care to avoid this kind of misleading statement:

> The poem is reminiscent of a happier time which the two
> lovers in it have associated with the park.

Ask yourself who is doing the reminiscing – the poem (or the lovers 'in it'), or the writer of the sentence? If we say 'The poem is reminiscent', it is the writer of the sentence who is doing the reminiscing. If, on the other hand, we say 'The poem reminisces', it is quite clearly the poem. The writer of this sentence clearly intends the second meaning, since he is not concerned with his own memories of the park but with those of the poet himself and of the lovers who are in the park.

Since much academic writing engages in the self-conscious analysis of what the writer says about what other writers have said, it is very easy to blur the distinction between self and other by an unwise choice of word or structure. But if you are clear in your own mind what it is *you* are doing, and if you resist the temptation to hide behind the texts of your sources, you should have little difficulty avoiding the kinds of confusion exemplified above.

3 Some verbs of enquiry: how to use them

We have already met many of the verbs you will use to express your own and other scholars' processes of enquiry (e.g. know, believe, analyse, see, observe, examine, find, show, describe, explain, define). For the most part the distinctions in meaning between these words do not cause us a great deal of trouble; we get into trouble with them – as we have seen – when we combine them with other elements in a sentence. There are, nevertheless, some verbs of enquiry whose meanings and uses often do cause considerable difficulty, partly because they are used fairly loosely in non-academic writing and speech. Below is a gloss on the uses of those that cause most difficulty.

Uninterested/disinterested

These words are not, strictly speaking, verbs, but let that pass. 'Disinterested' has recently colonised that part of the map of meaning once occupied by 'uninterested', but in the process has lost its own distinct identity. The traditional distinction between these words probably oversimplifies the relations between self and subject matter; it will nevertheless be passionately adhered to by many of your tutors.

'Uninterested' has been reserved to express one's lack of interest in enquiring into a subject at all. You will probably have studied some subject, found it not interesting to you and given it away at the first opportunity. To say that you are uninterested, therefore, is merely to state a subjective or idiosyncratic aversion, a point of view which is of no relevance to academic enquiry. To express your disinterest, on the other hand, is to affirm an objectivity which says that you are ready to make your judgements on the evidence and arguments available and to change your mind if necessary. Lack of interest will show in whether you engage with a subject in the first place (it is better not to choose essay topics in which you are uninterested – see chapter 2, section 2); disinterest will show in your attitude to the *outcome* of your enquiry into a topic.

Imply/infer

This is another distinction to whose preservation many of your tutors will be passionately devoted. For the most part it is a useful one, even though there are times when it can quite legitimately be blurred, and even though (as *The Oxford English Dictionary* shows) such scholars as Milton and James Mill have ignored it.

You, as a scholar, can both imply and infer. If you imply something you imply it *to* your reader, and your reader infers it *from* your text. If, on the other hand, you infer, your inference is made either from a text you are reading or from data you are examining. If your inference is a legitimate one, then it might be said that the text or the author of the text implied what you say it did. Inferring, therefore, is a function of someone's reading and interpreting of texts and evidence; implying is a function of writing. You might use either word in the appropriate way to make much the same point:

Sabine's account of Burke implies [to me] that, rather than rejecting natural rights, Burke completely absorbed them into his notion of the conventional rights embodied in a 'civil society'.

I infer from Sabine's account of Burke that . . .

Feel

Treat 'feel' with great caution. It is often used by students in such a way that the 'feeling' cannot be justified in any public way. In writing about the arts (literature, music, painting, sculpture, etc.) 'feel' is used and can be used, but try not to use it merely as an affective substitute for 'think'.

Speculate/conjecture

Speculation and conjecture are often coupled with 'mere' by people of a wholly practical or empirical turn of mind. Speculation is a perfectly legitimate academic activity, as necessary as imagination, even to the most methodologically precise and experimental of disciplines. Speculating and conjecturing are not the exclusive preserve of mystics and poets, but may be engaged in whenever knowledge is sought. Chapter 2 of this book is largely about how to speculate. *The Oxford English Dictionary* quotes Dickens's *Our Mutual Friend* to convey the opprobrium attached to speculation: 'His knowledge of its affairs was mostly speculative and all wrong.' Coleridge, at times a speculative thinker himself, puts the other side of the case: 'A certain number of speculative minds is necessary to a cultivated state of society.' The utilitarian J. S. Mill includes his treatise *Representative Government* in the category 'speculations concerning forms of government', declaring that 'speculative thought is one of the chief elements of social power'. The charge to avoid is not 'mere speculation' but 'idle speculation'.

Imagine

Most worthwhile knowledge is achieved by what Jacob Bronowski has called 'a creative leap of the imagination' rather than by a set of discovery procedures. What was necessary for Einstein is necessary for us. The ability to imagine 'possible worlds' is a necessary accomplishment in many disciplines: for example, by trying to imagine what is not the case, what could not be the case, or what might be the case, we are led to appreciate more clearly what is the case. Even historians – with their traditional distaste for historical 'ifs' – have tried to assess the economic significance of the spread of the railroads in nineteenth-century America by imagining what the economy would have been like *without* them. Only vacant and idle imaginings are to be rejected.

Wish/hope

No attitude to one's material can be founded only on wishes or hopes. Consequently, these verbs will more commonly be used in combination with others conveying a sense of certainty or assertion, for example 'I hope to demonstrate that . . . ', 'I wish to acknowledge that . . . '.

4 Quoting – and not quoting

Whether you should quote from other sources in your essays, and when you should do it, are questions particularly relevant to the success with which you establish a satisfactory relationship between your language and your material. Tutors in the humanities and social sciences are not impressed by scissors-and-paste essays which consist largely of quotations stitched together by a few linking sentences and paragraphs. Here is one tutor's comment on an essay that has quoted too much: 'You quote fairly extensively from different secondary sources but you allow what you say to govern the drift of your essay to the point where you can't hold a consistent line of your own.' If you quote excessively you are allowing the words of somebody else to choke off your own chances of coming to understand and interpret the material. Your essay cannot then be your own best answer.

You might most frequently be tempted to quote when you feel

you have not sufficiently understood the meaning of your material and cannot find words of your own to express the idea. When this happens you should try to apply the techniques of reading and note-taking set out in chapter 3, particularly those in the section 'Interpreting a difficult text'. Your aim is to create a 'compound' from elements of your own language and that of the sources you are using.

If it is important to use your own language as much as possible with difficult texts and ideas, there is rarely any justification for presenting straightforward facts or general, uncontroversial information in the form of quotations from your sources. DESCRIBING things, events and situations you will probably have practised more than any other kind of writing; so even though you might at times find it difficult to work out how best to describe coherently some complex set of events and the relationships between them, you should nevertheless resist the temptation to quote one more or less randomly chosen author's account.

The best justification for quoting is the presentation of such primary data or evidence as you then go on to analyse, for example experimental results, the answers to survey questions, a table of raw figures or statistics, lines from a literary work, a statement from some primary historical document. Quoting is a way of putting before your reader the object to be discussed, just as you might get out a family photograph to point to, when some discussion about it takes place.

The opinions and interpretations of the writers of secondary sources may be used in much the same way. We quote them not to save us the bother of rendering their ideas in our own words, or merely to appeal to the authority of the author. Rather, we quote so that we can say to our reader: 'This is what so-and-so says. What does she mean? How well does the evidence support her opinion? I agree (or disagree) with her point of view because . . .', and so on. It is probably true to say that academic authors quote the opinions of others when they want to challenge that opinion more often than when they want to accede to it.

Finally, quotations may also be used if an author has expressed a point particularly clearly, succinctly or elegantly. I have done this at the beginning of the chapters in this book. Such enhancement of your own writing can be a good idea, so long as the quotation is apt. But, unlike an after-dinner speech, its value to an academic essay lies in its sparing use. To indulge yourself too often in the quoting of others' great thoughts is to run the risk of never learning to formulate your own.

8
Analytical language 1: sentences

The world was made before the
English language, and seemingly
upon a different design.

ROBERT LOUIS STEVENSON

1 Discrimination and confusion

The quotation above expresses one writer's rueful admission that
there is nothing easy or natural about getting the English language (or any other, for that matter) to constitute adequately
what the world is like. The language has to be pushed and coaxed,
stretched and compressed, chiselled and hammered to get it to
match the reality you are trying to make sense of. It is common to
talk about 'polishing' your language – like a diamond – as if that is
all you have to do. But before that the diamond has to be mined
and cut. This is the hardest part. As T. S. Eliot says:

> Words strain,
> Crack and sometimes break, under the burden,
> Under the tension, slip, slide, perish . . .
> ('Burnt Norton' in *Four Quartets*)

When they do these things we easily become confused and,
hence, what we are writing about becomes confused and not
always easily understood by a reader.

In this chapter we are going to examine some of the confu-
sions that can arise when we try to combine words into sentences. It is the province of grammar to help us discriminate
between making sense and engendering confusion when we
combine words. It also helps us to discriminate between senses

or meanings we intend and those we don't, for example in the elimination of unwanted ambiguities. This chapter is therefore about certain aspects of English grammar.

You will not find in the pages that follow a comprehensive guide to the grammar of English. It takes a whole book to do that. What you will find are just a few pointers designed to help you to recognise and to preempt some of the confusions that might creep into your own academic writing.

Some of these confusions, you might find, only become a problem when you are writing academic essays. It is sometimes the case that students discover they cannot consistently write grammatical sentences only when they begin a university or college course. Others find problems begin to arise only in the second or third year of their course. If either of these things happens to you, the cause is probably the extra demands placed on your understanding by more complex, more subtle or more abstract ideas. You might need to give your language a chance to catch up with your growing understanding. Structuring sentences, which, early in the year, can be causing you many problems, could well begin to right itself as you become clearer about what it is you are trying to say. Even so, by studying the pointers to sentence structures and processes contained in this chapter, you can make yourself aware of some of the pitfalls to look out for.

Yet other students find that their ability to structure sentences collapses in just one or two of the subjects they are studying. If you find your English expression is praised by the geography tutor and severely criticised by the tutor in sociology or in history, it might well be that you are finding it harder to make sense of the ideas or methods of enquiry practised in sociology or history. It is also the case that disciplines vary somewhat in the kinds of distinction they make use of. It is therefore quite easy to write confused sentences until the nature of the relevant distinctions is pointed out to you. We cannot here cover all the sources of grammatical confusion that might arise in the arts and social sciences. There is, however, something you can do for yourself.

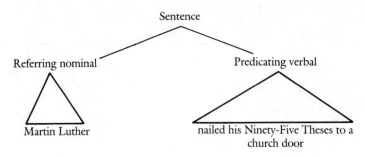

Figure 5

If a tutor writes 'Confused' – and no more – in the margin of your essay, make a special effort to have the precise nature of the confusion explained to you. It is important to you, and it doesn't do the tutor any harm to have to articulate the problem.

2 Elements of sentence structure

2.1 *Referring and predicating*

The first distinction you must be able to draw is the one that underlies the structure of most of the sentences you will write. Academic language (perhaps more than other kinds) engages in making statements or propositions. Logical propositions and the declarative sentences (or statements) based on them have two main parts: (a) a NOMINAL (naming) expression which REFERS to some object, idea or entity in the world; and (b) a VERBAL expression which PREDICATES of these nominals some action, process, situation or relation. That is to say, something we want to write about is identified by giving it a name (referring), and then we go on to say something about it (predicating). Making sense of the world demands that some statement about it combines these nominal referring expressions and predicating verbals. This structure is represented in Figure 5.

Now, nominals and verbals are not easily distinguished

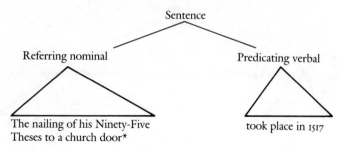

Figure 6

according to the kinds of entities they express. Both include non-physical entities such as states, situations, actions, events, processes, relations, and so on. Rather, it is the *functions* of referring and predicating that distinguish them. An action, for example, that might be a verbal predicator in one sentence (as in Figure 5) may, with some slight but important grammatical changes, become part of a nominal referring expression in another (see Figure 6). The underlying structure therefore remains the same. The fact that we have incorporated the verbal of the first sentence into the nominal of the second requires us to find a new predicating verbal ('took place in 1517') with which to complete the structure.

The predicating verbal usually needs to contain what is called a 'finite verb' (e.g. nailed, took place), as opposed to a 'non-finite verb' (e.g. nailing, to nail, taking place, to take place). The term 'finite' here means 'limited' or 'restricted'. Perhaps the easiest way to recognise whether a verb is finite is to see whether it is limited in respect of its *tense* – past, present or future. The non-finite (infinitive) form with 'to' (e.g. to nail) is tenseless. In this sentence 'to nail' is part of the nominal referring expression and has nothing to do with the predicate:

> To nail the Ninety-Five Theses on a Wittenberg church door was a calculated political act.

* Notice that, even when the referring nominal is an extended one like this, there is no need for a comma between the nominal and the verbal.

Like the 'to' infinitive the '-ing' form of the verb (e.g. nailing) is non-finite unless it is preceded by certain auxiliary verbs that do carry tense. These auxiliaries are forms of the verb 'be' (am, is, are, was, were), the verb 'have' (has, have, had) and the so-called modal verbs (e.g. shall–should, will–would, can–could, may–might, must, ought). In Figure 6 there is no tense in the 'nailing' of the referring nominal, whilst 'took place' in the predicating verbal is in the past tense. It is the absence of a predicating verbal carrying tense in the second 'sentence' below which makes it unacceptable in formal academic English:

> In 1517 Martin Luther performed a calculated political act.
> Nailing his Ninety-Five Theses to a church door in
> Wittenberg.

To be able to discriminate between these two major constituents of a simple declarative sentence – the referring nominal and the predicating verbal with its finite verb marked for tense – is absolutely necessary if you are to follow some of the complications and exceptions introduced below. It is also necessary if you are to avoid the kinds of common confusion we shall examine later in this chapter. The reason for this is simply that many of the choices of vocabulary and grammatical structure you make in the referring nominal determine the choices available to you in the predicate (or vice versa). If these choices do not match, your writing becomes ungrammatical and confused.

2.2 Sentences without finite verbs

We saw above an example of a piece of language which cannot be called a sentence because it lacks a predicating verbal. Here is another:

> Luther did not think the papacy or an ecclesiastical elite could
> determine faith. Faith being dispersed throughout the
> community of the faithful.

It can easily be fixed, either by incorporating the fragment into the first sentence,

> Luther did not think the papacy or an ecclesiastical elite could determine faith, faith being dispersed throughout the community of the faithful.

or by simply changing the non-finite 'being dispersed' to the finite 'is dispersed':

> Luther did not think the papacy or an ecclesiastical elite could determine faith. Faith (he thought) is dispersed throughout the community of the faithful.

There are, nevertheless, certain conditions under which the finite verb, or even the referring nominal, can be dispensed with. The first condition is that the finite form can be recovered from a verb in the preceding sentence either by repeating it or by using a substitute. Examples of substitutes are 'do' for an action, 'happen' for an event and 'be' for a state or situation. To repeat the verb or to use a substitute leads not only to unnecessary redundancy but also to the insertion of rather meaningless nominals to complete the syntactic structure:

> Quaker society was not rigidly stratified in the sense that one social layer was sharply marked off from its neighbours. Quite the reverse. In the 'Society of Friends' the bonds of employer and employee were close.

The second of these sentences is wholly grammatical because the omitted verb 'was' is recoverable from the first sentence. To add in the verb would, further, have required one of those relatively meaningless words like 'situation' or 'case' which add nothing of substance to the idea being expressed:

> The situation was quite the reverse.

> Quite the reverse was the case.

An illustration of how substitute verbs can be recoverable from the preceding sentence is this:

> Did Luther seek to avoid a confrontation with the Emperor Charles V? Nothing of the sort. He worked hard to bring it about.

'Nothing of the sort' could be expanded to 'He did nothing of the sort' or, perhaps, 'Nothing of the sort took place'. The verbless sentence is more effective than either of these. The examples of verbless sentences above illustrate the second condition that such sentences should fulfil in academic writing: they are best used as a transitional comment summing up the writer's attitude to what has gone before or to what follows.

You will find many examples of sentences without finite verbs in novels, journalism and popular writing. (They are discussed by Ernest Gowers under the entry 'Verbless sentences' in the second edition of Fowler's *Modern English Usage*.) Most of these are not appropriate to academic writing. The style of certain detective novels, for example, in which particular prominence is given to circumstances of place and time is feeble in academic prose:

> Luther declared his opposition to the sale of indulgences. In his Ninety-Five Theses. In Wittenberg. On the church door.

This kind of writing is at odds with what an academic essay should probably be emphasising – the main proposition, contained in the first sentence, rather than the circumstances of time and place.

2.3 Conjoining clauses into complex sentences

Conjunctions and sentence adverbials

A sentence which consists of a single nominal, referring expression and a predicating verbal expression is also said to constitute a single 'main clause'. A main clause asserts the principal proposition of a sentence. We can add further propositions to a sentence by adding to the main clause or embedding within it various other kinds of clause. It is the function of these clauses to EXTEND, ELABORATE and ENHANCE the main proposition, very much in the way we saw these processes operating in chapter 5, section 3. That is to say, they have these functions: to add on new information; to provide exceptions and alternatives;

to clarify, substantiate and exemplify the main proposition; or to enhance it by imposing such circumstantial restrictions as time, place, manner, means, cause, condition and concession on its truth and range of application. You can probably handle many of the structural problems posed by these compound and complex sentences. There are, however, a few which do commonly cause difficulty. To these we now turn.

The first general point to keep in mind is that certain kinds of word must normally be employed when you want to attach extra clauses to the main clause. The most common of these are called 'conjunctions' since they conjoin clauses. Examples are 'and', 'but', 'or', 'whereas', 'because', 'so that', 'if' and 'although'. Conjunctions are to be distinguished from another class of words whose meanings are similar but whose grammatical use is quite different. These latter (called 'sentence adverbials' or 'linking terms') do not join together clauses in the same sentence; rather, they provide the links of thought and meaning between quite separate sentences. Examples are 'furthermore', 'on the other hand', 'by contrast', 'alternatively', 'for this reason', 'therefore' and 'however'. Whether we choose to write longer sentences whose clauses are joined by conjunctions or shorter sentences linked by sentence adverbials is often simply a matter of style and emphasis (see chapter 10).

What we cannot usually do is to join clauses by means of sentence adverbs or link sentences by means of conjunctions. (The exceptions to this rule are the coordinating conjunctions 'and', 'or' and 'but', which may be used to begin a new sentence.) However common it may be in informal writing, this kind of language will be regarded with disfavour by most of your tutors:

> Martin Luther nailed his Ninety-Five Theses to the church door in Wittenberg. Because he wanted to make a political statement which would draw the Elector of Saxony's support.

> Luther wanted to secure the Elector of Saxony's support for his Theses, therefore he nailed them to the church door in Wittenberg.

Luther was successful in gaining the Elector's support, however, he overestimated the latter's ability to protect him.

The elector of Saxony supported Luther. Whereas most of the rulers of German states succumbed to the pressure of the Emperor Charles V.

Punctuation: colons and semi-colons

There are two important qualifications to this. Both involve using those punctuation marks, the semi-colon (;) and colon (:), that you might feel unsure about. Sentence adverbials, as in the second and third examples above, can be used to conjoin clauses into a single complex sentence if that join is made with a semi-colon in place of the comma. The semi-colon is the super-glue which can hold together almost any pair of statements whose subject matter is related; it can even be used if the nature of that relation is not made explicit by a sentence adverbial.

The colon, by contrast, indicates a relation of a certain kind: one between a general and a particular statement. In the sentence below the first statement mentions 'a calculated political act'; the second specifies the particular nature of that act:

In 1517 Luther performed a calculated political act: he nailed his Ninety-Five Theses to a church door in Wittenberg.

You are probably familiar with this use of the colon in slightly different contexts: when in your lecture notes you make a general heading, to be followed by more specific statements; or when in an essay you make a general statement and follow it with a quotation to make your point concrete and particular. To sum up, you can use the colon when ELABORATING a point, as we saw in chapter 5 (pp. 117–22), namely to CLARIFY, to SUBSTAN-TIATE and to EXEMPLIFY.

There is a kind of complex sentence structurally somewhat different from those we have looked at, but which expresses a relationship similar to that signalled by the colon. In this structure the main clause consists – as usual – of a nominal referring expression and a predicating verb ('Luther argued' in the example below). The verb expresses perception (observe, see, hear, etc.). An extra clause is added to this main clause by using 'that', and so is informally called a 'that' clause:

> At the Diet of Worms in 1521 Luther argued that only Scripture and reason could be used to prove him wrong.

The connection with the use of the colon should be quite obvious. The 'that' clause specifies what Luther argued, a paraphrase of what he actually said:

> Luther argued: 'it is impossible for me to recant unless I am proved wrong by the testimony of Scripture or by evident reasoning.'

Notice one thing about the punctuation of this structure. In modern English there is no comma either before or after the 'that'. Do not write: 'Luther argued, that only Scripture . . .'; or 'Luther argued that, only Scripture . . .'.

We are not now going to look any further into the purely formal structures of declarative sentences. Despite the various quali-fications we have noticed above, it remains the case, first, that the fundamental structure of any sentence you write needs to reflect those complementary functions of referring and predicating. You can help yourself make this distinction if you can also learn to distinguish between a finite verb – which specifies the tense of your statement – and a non-finite form of the verb. Once you are clear about this, you can in very particular circumstances modify your sentence structures by deleting certain elements. And then, secondly, you can complicate simple sentences by adding further clauses with the aid of conjunctions, semi-colons and colons. To be able to manage these things will not guarantee that you will always write well-structured, grammatical sentences. But it will help to underpin your ability to avoid certain other sources of confusion in their design. These last are perhaps more obviously connected with structuring meanings. So to potential confu-sions of meaning in structuring our sentences we now turn.

3 Participants, processes and circumstances

We have learned to distinguish the functions of referring and predicating when we construct our sentences. We shall now look at the sentence and the clause from a slightly different point of view – the combining and manipulating of their elements to express how the world we write about is ordered or how it might be ordered.

We make sense of the world, both to ourselves and to our readers, by exploring the various PROCESSES that go on in it – actions, events, situations, perceptions, relations of various kinds, and so on. We also seek to identify the various phenomena that take part in these processes. The phenomena most closely studied in the humanities are people – the abstract ideas, the social structures and institutions, the works of art and the languages they create, as well as aspects of the natural world in which they live. These phenomena we shall call PARTICIPANTS in the various kinds of process mentioned above. For example, dogs (participants) bark (an action); politicians get elected (an event); people own houses (a relationship of possession between two participants, people and houses); and scholarship is difficult (a relationship which ascribes a characteristic to the participant).

In addition, participants engage in these processes in certain restricted CIRCUMSTANCES of time, place, manner, means, condition, concession, causation, intention, etc., which often need to be made explicit. So, dogs bark *when* they are alarmed; politicians *in* ideal democracies get elected *by* appealing success-fully to the electorate; people own houses *if* they can afford to *and if* the government allows the private holding of dwellings; scholarship remains difficult *despite* the assistance of modern information technology.

Now, it is from our study of the world and its representation in language that we learn how to combine various participants with various processes and circumstances in ways that make sense. We should not ordinarily write that scholarship gets elected by painting landscapes, that dogs own houses in order to abolish equilibrium, or that houses own people under a kilo-gram of kinship ties. Statements like these look like nonsense, the nonsense arising from the coupling of incompatible partici-pants, processes and circumstances. On the other hand, we might well write that politicians both bark at and bite each other, that a dog's obeyed in office, and that these dogs control the House by means of their whips. Since language slips and slides about (as it does in these last examples) the line between sense and nonsense can be quite fuzzy and difficult to clarify, especially when you are embarking on the study of some subject quite new to you: it becomes quite easy to lump together in sentences categories of participants and processes that are kept quite distinct in the various disciplines you might be studying. What we shall do now is examine some of the commoner problems that arise when we confuse some of the processes, participants and circumstances studied in the arts and social sciences.

3.1 Clarifying participants, human and non-human

It might seem unlikely that you would say things of human participants that can only properly be said of non-humans, or vice versa. Yet this is routinely done. At times it is quite accept-able. We use metaphor: 'A *dog's* obeyed in office.' We use metonymy, personification and other devices by which an inanimate object can substitute for a human or human institu-tion: 'The power of the English *crown* was whittled away in the century following the 1688 revolution'; '*1688* saw the beginnings of constitutional monarchy'. These ways of expressing the world come so naturally to us that we would think absurdly literal anyone who pointed out, for example, that the year 1688 can actually 'see' nothing at all.

Similarly, there are some processes which allow the partici-pant which carries them out to be either human or non-human, but upon which there are restrictions on the kind of participant that may be affected by the process. The first of these participants (the one who 'does') we can call the 'actor'. The second we can call the 'affected':

> With his discovery of the mathematical laws of perspective, Brunelleschi opened the door to modern realist painting.

> The door to modern realist painting opened with Brunelleschi's discovery of the mathematical laws of perspective.

In the first sentence the non-human door is the participant affected by the process of opening, and Brunelleschi is the actor. In the second sentence, the door has become the actor in this process. 'Open' is one of the verbs which allow this switch of human and non-human actor to take place.

In most processes, by contrast, it is quite unacceptable to substitute the non-human for the human actor. Discovery is one such process: Brunelleschi might be either the actor who discovers or the affected who is discovered; but the laws of perspective cannot do the discovering. Discovery, like all those processes of perceiving and enquiring that figure so centrally in academic writing, is generally attributed only to intelligent, sentient minds.

The student who wrote the sentence below has quite confused the participants and processes involved in the study of history:

> Documentary evidence unearths the reasons behind events in searching for better historical explanations.

What kind of participant engages in the processes of unearthing and searching for things in academic activities of the kind being written about here? The answer will be the enquirer, in this case the historian, who is not mentioned. This sentence says it is the documentary evidence. (You will notice an example here of a dangling modifier, 'in searching ...', discussed in the previous chapter.) Moreover, it is the documentary evidence which is the participant affected by the unearthing, rather than the reasons. That is to say, the documentary evidence is what is 'unearthed'; the reasons why we should explain events in one way rather than another are provided by the historian. That, at any rate, is one of the uses of the word 'reason' by historians. Perhaps the writer half had in mind yet another participant not mentioned at all: the historical figures who had their reasons for initiating the events being enquired into.

So what have become lost in this sentence are the distinctions between quite a number of things:

- human participants performing an action, that is the historical enquirer unearthing documents and searching for better explanations;
- non-human participants on which the action is performed, that is the documents unearthed;
- both human (the people) and non-human (the events) participants which constitute the subject matter of the documents;
- the reasons given by historians to justify their explanations;
- the reasons given by historical figures for the events they took part in.

Here are a few attempts to get into the writer's mind and work out what she was trying to say:

Historians seek better explanations of events by unearthing documents which provide new evidence of the reasons historical figures gave for their actions.

Historians use documentary evidence the better to justify their explanations of historical events.

Documents contain the evidence of the reasons for events which historians need when searching for better historical explanations.

There are other possibilities. Notice, first, that they mean different things. Hence, if you suspect that you have written a sentence which seems to have confused a number of different participants and processes, you must do your best to work out which of the various meanings you really intend. Your answer will depend largely on the context in which the sentence arises – what you have already written so far. In our example, the writer should probably have looked back through her paragraph to decide – in the first instance – whether she was writing about (human) historians, about (inanimate) documents or, indeed, about the evidence contained in the documents. Once the topic is selected from options such as these, it may be made the nominal referring expression in the main clause of the sentence, and the rest of the options in meaning and structure must then be selected to fit in with that starting point.

3.2 Concrete and abstract

Processes expressed in abstract nouns

We have hitherto tended to assume that the processes in which our participants take part are usually expressed in the form of finite and non-finite verbs. That is not the whole story. There are many processes which are expressed in referring nouns or in nominals which have been formed from verbs. Most of them are quite easy to recognise. Sometimes there is no change or little change in the form of the word (e.g. study–study, rise–rise, believe–belief, grow–growth). More often '-ing', '-ation' (or '-tion'), '-ment', '-al' or '-age' is affixed to the end of the verb to make the nominal (e.g. thinking, organisation, adoption, arrangement, dismissal, wastage). These are formed from the verbs 'think', 'organise', 'adopt', 'arrange', 'dismiss' and 'waste'. Now, these nouns refer to processes, just as verbs express processes. And like verbs, a participant is associated with them, even if it isn't expressed explicitly in the sentence. Somebody or something performs the study, the growth, the thinking, the organisation, the adoption, and so on.

If we employ the abstract style of writing (especially common in sociological and political writing as well as in much recent linguistics and literary criticism) we get sentences littered with abstract nominalisations of processes:

> The utilisation of the concept of underdevelopment requires
> firstly a recognition that it is based on the concept of a
> dialectical relationship between the development of the First
> World and the underdevelopment of the Third World.

One of the reasons why this kind of writing is difficult for many
people to follow is that rarely are the participants ever made
explicit. In this statement it is we (the enquirers) who do the
utilising and the recognising, whilst the developing and under-
developing is the responsibility of an undefined abstraction. It is
easy to be tempted by the books you read into imitating this kind
of language. But it is a language quite difficult to control, even
for the experts. The sentence above can be made to bring the
participants to the surface, for example:

> If we are to use the concept of underdevelopment, we must
> first recognise that it is based on a dialectical relationship
> between how capitalists have developed the First World and
> how this necessarily entails that the Third World remains
> underdeveloped.

Now, there is nothing ungrammatical about the original version
of this statement. It is, simply, harder to understand until you
have become practised in 'translating' this kind of language into
a version somewhat like that immediately above.

But this mode of thinking can cause another kind of problem.
If you are not practised in the handling of processes that have
been nominalised and made abstract, it is very easy to make
grammatical mistakes:

> Salisbury considers that the Pacific islanders gained from the
> introduction to steel tools.

'Introduction', you will recognise, expresses a nominalised
process of the kind we have been discussing. You will see that
there is something funny about the phrase 'the introduction to
steel tools'. Now, if you ask the question 'Who introduced steel
tools and whom were they introduced to?', you find that there

are two participants involved, not just the one made explicit in the sentence: the unidentified participant is (presumably) the Western trader; and the second the Pacific islander. Which of these two participants does the writer wish to concentrate on? To choose the one or the other requires a different sentence structure:

> Salisbury considers that the Pacific islanders gained from *the* [traders'] introduction *of* steel tools.

or:

> Salisbury considers that the Pacific islanders gained from *their* introduction *to* steel tools.

A similar mistake has been made by the writer of this sentence:

> Hyndman had the belief of respect of social order.

The participants associated with 'belief' and 'respect' are quite different – Hyndman (an English socialist writer) and socialists. And like the previous example, this one contains a grammatical mistake with a preposition ('to' in the earlier one, 'of' in this). The best way to make this sentence both clear and grammatical is to use verbs to represent the processes, a change which makes the participants quite clear:

> Hyndman believed that socialists should respect social order.

From these examples a useful warning emerges. When you are reading back over the sentences you have written, look out for the structure 'the' + abstract noun, where the noun refers to a process. Always satisfy yourself that the participant associated with each process is quite clear from the context, that it has not changed in mid-sentence, and that you have not made a mistake with any preposition you have used (to, of, at, in, with, by, from, etc.). If you are in doubt, try rewriting the sentence in such a way that the processes are expressed as verbs rather than as abstract nouns.

Noun–verb agreement

If the noun you use to refer to a participant is abstract, then the process must be represented by a verb which is compatible with an abstract noun. In this sentence the major participant, architecture, is abstract:

> The architecture of the Indus valley was built with a strong sense of form and mass.

One builds buildings, not architecture. So we must decide whether it is the abstract or the concrete we wish to write about:

> The architecture of the Indus valley displays a strong sense of form and mass.

or:

> The buildings of the Indus valley were constructed with a strong sense of form and mass.

Similarly, one cannot in certain contexts 'use' landscapes. One can use land or one can change landscapes:

> There have been changes in the use of landscape in the city of Moorabbin.

'Landscape' (as it is used in geography – unlike one of its uses in art) is abstract; 'land' is concrete. So we might say either:

> There have been changes in the use of land in the city of Moorabbin.

or:

> There have been changes in the landscape in the city of Moorabbin.

Abstract processes are easy to confuse with concrete participants:

> These differing interest groups were brought to a head by the Corn Law question.

What are 'differing interest groups'? We might say:

> The differences between these interest groups were brought to a head by the Corn Law question.

or:

> These differing interest groups clashed over the Corn Law question.

or:

> These groups differed on the Corn Law question.

Differences can be brought to a head; or interest groups can clash.

It is not easy to lay down general rules about what is abstract and what is concrete, or about which nouns can be coupled with which verbs. The borderlines between abstract and concrete nouns can be difficult to discern and may vary with the discipline being studied. If you are in doubt, it is probably safer to err on the side of concreteness in your choice both of participants and processes. In any case, check with a good dictionary, in particular a specialist dictionary in the relevant discipline.

3.3 Texts, words and things

The function of quotation marks and underlining

What can be said about phenomena in the world cannot necessarily be said about the texts which deal with them or about the words in those texts. Nor, conversely, can some statements about words or about texts be couched in language designed to talk about other kinds of phenomenon. By omitting inverted commas around the first word, this sentence, for example, does not discriminate sufficiently between the word and the phenomenon it refers to:

> Ambivalence consists of four syllables.

The result is both nonsensical and untrue.

If you are a student of literature, in particular, you must

constantly decide whether what you want to say is about the words in the texts or about the phenomena these words represent. For example, in Conrad's novel *Heart of Darkness*, the word 'darkness' is used a great deal with varying shades of meaning. Anybody writing about this novel must take care to distinguish between Conrad's deployment of the word in his text and the ideas of mystery, the unconscious, lack of understanding, sin, the jungle, absence of civilisation, and so on, which it conjures up.

Similarly, the convention of underlining (or italicising) the names of texts must be followed if you are to avoid writing sentences like this one, in which it is not immediately clear whether the participant is Hamlet the character or *Hamlet* the play:

> The central dramatic question posed by Hamlet is not 'Why did Hamlet seek revenge?' but 'Why didn't Hamlet avenge his father?'

It is the play, not the character, which poses the 'dramatic question', a question which Hamlet himself cannot answer since he is only one part of the drama. Hamlet poses questions of a somewhat different kind – for example 'Am I a coward?' (II, ii, 606) – which might constitute just part of the evidence you could call on in your own answer to the larger dramatic question posed by the play as a whole. You will see, then, that the underlining of titles and the enclosing within quotation marks of quotations and references to words is more than just another inexplicable convention of academic writing. It marks the difference between two quite separate categories of experience.

It is not just literature students who must deal with texts and the differences between words and things. The texts of both primary and secondary sources in any discipline constitute verbal evidence with which your own analytical writing must deal. It is therefore important that you think carefully before assuming that there is no distinction to be made between what a source is talking about and the words in which the idea is couched. To help you appreciate this distinction and to use it in your writing, it is often valuable to compare the accounts of the same thing given by different authors. You will remember that in chapter 3 we conducted such an exercise on three different accounts of the opening to Kant's *Critique of Pure Reason*. We found that one of these writers was unique (and misleading) in his use of the word 'stimulus' to interpret Kant. What Kant must have had in mind has nothing to do with stimuli or responses.

Object-language and meta-language

Finally, there is a large vocabulary of terms especially character-istic of academic writing which is used to refer to the partici-pants and processes of academic enquiry itself – what we call a 'meta-language'. These terms have already been made much use of in this book, so you will be familiar with many of them. They include all those terms which express what academic authors and enquirers DO, introduced in earlier chapters, for example:

> proposing, acceding, conceding, refuting, dismissing,
> reconciling, describing, comparing, defining, explaining,
> theorising, justifying, evaluating, extending, elaborating,
> enhancing, generalising, particularising.

Then, there are many other nouns and nominals associated with these activities, for example:

> fact, evidence, data, idea, concept, conjecture, thesis,
> hypothesis, theory, opinion, belief, judgement, observations,
> findings, result, explanation, reason, argument, conclusion.

To be able to combine terms such as these into grammatical sentences is a skill that does not always come easily, and often takes time. (For this reason you should pay careful attention to how they are used in the books you read.) But there is one pitfall you must try to avoid from the very start – the confusing of these 'meta-linguistic' terms with the object or objects of your enquiry:

> This fact has a marked effect on ground temperatures.

Facts belong to the world of enquiry and thought. Such things cannot affect natural phenomena like ground temperatures. This should be quite easy to see. Here is a somewhat more difficult one:

> Pluralists argue that power is widely dispersed throughout society. This is very idealistic. In the real world this argument contains many loopholes due to the complicated structure of the economic and political system. However, there are situations in today's political climate where this line of reasoning does exist.

The argument doesn't contain loopholes in the real world, but in the 'meta-world' of arguments. Similarly, the pluralist line of reasoning doesn't so much 'exist' in today's political climate; rather, it can be *applied* to account for that climate. What we must do is to construct our sentences in such a way that the relationship between arguments and the 'real world' of politics is made more secure. If you get into the kind of situation that has troubled the writer of this passage, you might decide, on the one hand, to focus more particularly on what happens in the world:

> Pluralists argue that power is widely dispersed throughout society. This argument is very idealistic. In the real world power is very unevenly distributed owing to the complicated structure of the economic and political system. However, there are situations in which we do find power to be well dispersed.

Alternatively, you might decide to focus on the qualities of the argument:

> Pluralists argue that political power is widely dispersed throughout society. This argument is very idealistic in that it oversimplifies the complexities of power distribution to be found in actual economic and political systems. However, it does give an accurate account of some parts of the system.

What you must always do your very best to avoid is mixing within the same sentence the words and structures appropriate to argument with those appropriate to the object or phenomenon the argument is about.

3.4 *Singular and plural*

Perhaps unlike some of the problems we have examined in this chapter, you probably have no difficulty discriminating between singular and plural. The rule is simple enough: in most instances nominals in the singular must be followed by verbals in the singular, and plurals by plurals. Nevertheless, for some reason many students fail to make their nominals and verbals agree in number often enough to make it seem as though this constitutes a problem; and even very competent writers can slip up if they do not check over their sentences carefully. You might find that you make mistakes with number when you are labouring mightily over other aspects of your meaning. So if you have found a passage particularly difficult to write, it is a good idea to check back over it just to make sure you haven't made slips with singulars and plurals.

It is easy to make a mistake when the referring nominal is separated from the verb by lots of other words:

> The *relations* between line, form, space, tone and colour to be found in a picture *is* very complex.

Secondly, take especial care if your singular nominal is of the kind which refers not to one specific individual but to any member of that class of individuals – the so-called 'generic' reference. In the sentence below 'The social worker' refers generically to any social worker and all social workers, not to a single identified individual. The writer of this sentence has therefore had this in mind rather than the needs of number agreement:

> The social worker do not compromise their own standards and values to suit any occasion.

It is likely that the desire to avoid language which specifies the sex of the social worker is also implicated in the error here, as you will see from the 'their'. 'Their' cannot be substituted for 'his' or 'her' without your checking back through the sentence to ensure that everything agrees.

Thirdly, if a singular referring nominal is followed immediately by an 'of' phrase with plural nominals, it is easy to be distracted by these plurals when you come to assign number to the verb. This is probably because the plurals are most immediately in one's mind:

> The *frequency* of exercises in the old composition manuals *suggest* that number agreement can be a problem for many writers.

It is not the exercises that suggest, but their frequency that suggests.

Finally, there is a smallish group of nouns (called nouns of multitude) which, when used in the singular, may be followed by a verb in the plural. An army, committee, government, community, peer group, party, tribe, fraternity or jury – to take some common examples – may be viewed either as a collection of many independent individuals or as a single united whole. If the former meaning is to be emphasised, the verb is plural, whereas the singular verb emphasises the corporate action or responsibility of the group:

> The jury have decided on their verdict.

> The jury has found him guilty.

> The European Economic Community, who have always had their disagreements on agricultural policy, do accept the need for a new funding formula.

> The European Economic Community does not hesitate to dump surplus farm products on international markets.

This chapter has been concerned principally with helping you to get the main elements of your sentences to cohere with one another in a unified structure. A structure of any kind, if it is to be a good one, must always be looked at as a whole. If you are uncertain about, or wish to change, any of the elements in a structure you are building, you must always look beyond the bothersome element itself. You need to consider the effects which the various options open to you at one point in the sentence will have on the design of the whole. This means looking at your sentences much in the way you look at a picture: not just a succession of individual bits linked into a chain, but as an arrangement of forms and ideas.

If you feel that one of your sentences is getting into a dreadful mess and you cannot sort it out, perhaps the best thing to do *first* is to look carefully at the referring nominal which constitutes the actor in the main clause. Debate with yourself whether this is really what you are trying to write about. You might have used a word which refers to an abstract, non-human participant when really what you want is a concrete, human one. Ask whether you are focusing rather on what someone has said or written about the subject than on the subject matter itself (so far as you can disentangle them). Indeed, ask whether you can clarify in your mind what the participant is at all, because if that is vague, the chances are the rest of the sentence has nothing to hang onto. And so on. Falling between two stools (abstract/concrete, human/non-human, singular/plural, etc.) is a very common cause of injuries to sentences. It helps greatly if you can recognise the stools and decide on which one to aim for.

9
Analytical language 2: rhetorical strategies

Who, or why, or which, or what,
Is the Akond of Swat?

EDWARD LEAR

1 Analysing versus describing

In your writing there will be a place for description. You will need to describe such objects of your attention as a painting, the kinship system of a particular society, the land forms of a stretch of country, a chain of historical events, and so on. You will also from time to time need to describe what the authors of your sources have said about the subject matter you are enquiring into. But in modern academic writing, it is generally true to say, description by itself is not enough. It must be used to serve the purposes of analysis – of reflecting upon the significance of the information, the data, the evidence and the arguments that you assemble in your attempt to answer the question raised by your topic. We have noted in an earlier chapter that one of the more common remarks tutors make on an essay is that it is 'Too descriptive' or that it 'Needs more analysis'. How can these criticisms be met?

We have already seen how important it is for your essay to establish a case and argue for it. This is the first and most important condition to be met if your writing is to be analytical. But it is not the only one. In chapter 5 we examined the ways in which the case can be expanded. Not only might you need more information, but you also need to consider exceptions and alternatives, clarify the meaning of statements and substantiate your generalisations. You need, furthermore, to enhance the value of your information by asking and answering a whole variety of questions, like: When? Where? Who? By whom? For whom? By what means or methods? To what degree? For what reason or purpose? With what effect? Under which conditions? The application of these strategies was exemplified by the passages on rural poverty in the Third World in chapter 5. It is by expanding on your descriptive information in these ways that your writing can begin to become analytic.

Thirdly, analytical writing is of a piece with the analytical quality of your reading. In chapter 3 we saw how asking questions about what writers of your books are DOING (and not doing) makes it possible to analyse and interpret their words. If we pay attention only to the 'content' of the Brinton text on pp. 68–72 above, we will be tempted to write a purely descriptive account of the economic condition of France before the Revolution:

> In pre-revolutionary France it was the government rather than the country as a whole which was poor. Manufacturing, agriculture, building and foreign trade were all showing great improvement at a time when the government could not find sufficient money to pay its expenses. Uncultivated land was reduced by a third in Melun; Rouen doubled its production of cloth; and foreign trade increased by almost 100,000,000 livres between 1774 and 1787. However, the wealth generated by this expansion was not evenly distributed through all classes of society (Brinton 1965: 29–31).

Alternatively, by attending to what Brinton is doing as well as to what he is saying, we can begin to display some of the features of analytical writing:

> In *dismissing* the claim by Labrousse that the Revolution was born of economic hardship, Brinton (1965: 29–31) *argues* that it was not France as a whole but merely the government which was poor. He *defends* this thesis by *pointing* to the considerable growth in manufacturing, agriculture, building and foreign

> trade which occurred in the period before the Revolution. But the *examples he gives* of such growth – the reduction in unproductive land in Melun, the doubling of cloth production in Rouen and the expansion of foreign trade by 100,000,000 livres between 1774 and 1787 – can be misleading. While Brinton *concedes* that the benefits of this economic growth were unevenly shared between the classes of society, the *question he neglects* is whether this growth was uniformly spread throughout the various regions of the country.

Finally, your ability to write analytical prose will depend on how well you bring to bear on your material certain CRITERIA of analysis and evaluation. Criteria are more or less conventional standards that we apply to the evidence and arguments presented to us by our sources. In principle, there is nothing particularly special about this. When you go shopping you routinely apply such general criteria as price, quality and appropriateness to your needs to help you analyse the wares on offer. In addition, you will have further, more specific criteria, the choice of which depends on the nature of the article you are seeking. Examples might be design, durability, compatibility with articles you already possess, adaptability to a variety of likely uses, authenticity of the manufacturer's label appearing on the item, and so on. You might also apply certain political and moral criteria: you might exclude items made in certain countries, in 'sweat-shop' factory conditions, or manufactured in part from wild-animal skins. Many of the criteria that inform academic analysis are not dissimilar from some of these.

Here are some of the more general criteria that are commonly applied:

- What is the RELEVANCE of this material to the issue now under discussion?
- How RELIABLE is this evidence for the particular point I am making?
- How VALID is this argument?
- How COMPATIBLE is the evidence or argument with what we already know?

- How CONSISTENT are the individual parts of this description with each other and with what we know about the whole?
- Is this explanation sufficiently COMPREHENSIVE to take into account the evidence we have? Is it so comprehensive that there is no way in which we can TEST it by observation or experiment?
- What are the IMPLICATIONS of this for other things we believe or which we know to be important? How SIGNIFICANT is it?

The questions in which the terms in capitals appear above are not the only ones that can be asked. Learning the meanings of the criteria and learning how to phrase suitable questions around them takes time and study. Although the criteria above are widely used, their meanings can be rather unstable. In particular, they can mean different things to different disciplines, and different things to different schools of thought within those disciplines. For example, in psychology 'valid' can mean something like 'this test measures what it purports to measure'; in logic it means 'this argument is well formed'. You must therefore look to your books and your teachers in the disciplines you are reading to find out what the terms mean and how they can be used in analytical writing. The same goes for a whole host of other criteria which may be very specific to a few disciplines or to a particular school of thought.

Here is a version of our paragraph based on the Brinton text. It makes explicit use of some of the general criteria listed above as well as a few of the more specific ones just referred to:

> In dismissing the claim by Labrousse that the French Revolution was born of economic hardship, Brinton (1965: 29–31) relies heavily on very few figures to demonstrate the extent of economic growth. We must concede that he offers his figures only as 'examples', and has made no attempt to be *comprehensive* in his coverage. Nevertheless, we must question whether they give such a *reliable* picture of the whole French economy as to justify Brinton's *authoritative* assertion that we can be 'very certain' about the country's increasing prosperity.

> In the first place, as he notes, France had only just begun to collect economic statistics, so it is unlikely that the collection procedures were *uniform* and likely that some results were *biased* by the aspirations of those who provided them to their masters. Secondly, eighteenth-century France was an overwhelmingly rural economy. If we are to avoid giving undue *weight* to the considerable increases in manufactures or foreign trade, we must determine what the *base-lines* for those increases were and *how significant a proportion* of the gross national product they represented.
>
> With respect to the first of these questions we find that . . .

This piece begins by analysing the Brinton text itself and then goes on to raise a number of speculative questions about what Brinton's own analysis tends to assume. The second (and subsequent) paragraphs would need to engage in a close analysis of whatever evidence could be found to help answer these questions.

You will notice that description has almost entirely disappeared from the paragraph above. The sectors of the economy and the actual figures given by Brinton are not reported. Readers of this paragraph not immediately familiar with the Brinton text must therefore rely on the very few hints given. An allusive analytical style like this, when unrelieved and unsupported by some concrete description, can become unreasonable in its demands upon the reader, as you will probably have found when wading through some of your books. Do not, therefore, be afraid to include descriptive passages in your writing. Only take care that they are designed to make your analyses clearer and more telling.

2 Defining

2.1 *The dynamics of a definition*

Defining is a rather more complicated business than our usual experience with a desk dictionary leads us to suspect. In his

Introduction to Logical Theory the logician P. F. Strawson tells us that defining is a process by which we 'deliberately fix the boundaries of some words in relation to those of other words'. In using the word 'deliberately' Strawson is following the advice of Humpty Dumpty in *Through the Looking Glass*, who told Alice: 'When *I* use a word … it means just what I choose it to mean … The question is … which is to be master – that's all.' One of the functions of analytical writing is to decide which meanings should be given to words and concepts that might prove important to a particular field of study. This is why (as we saw in chapter 2, pp. 37–8) dictionary definitions of such words are not usually very helpful. You will find pages, not infrequently whole books, given over to an attempt to define difficult terms like 'justice', 'knowledge', 'class', or 'culture'. The result is that we do not have fixed and unchanging notions about the right or wrong meanings of such words, but rather CONCEPTIONS or THEORIES of justice, knowledge, class and culture, theories which are strenuously debated. Humpty Dumpty was arrogant only to the degree that he thought he could decide the meaning of a word quite on his own account.

Strawson's definition of definition (which, you will now realise, summarises a theory of definition) also refers to fixing the boundaries of words. That is to say it 'limits' or 'defines' those boundaries. How is this done? When you set out to define something you will need to decide on the CRITERIA you will use in order to delimit where those boundaries will be. In this way, as you will see, defining things is just another kind of analysis. As with other kinds of analysis, you will need to learn the kinds of criteria each discipline you study applies to the definition of terms.

There is one fundamental distinction, however, which is common to all our attempts to define. This is the distinction between criteria that do make possible the fixing of boundaries and those that do not. These are called 'defining' and 'non-defining' criteria. (The distinction is important for certain aspects of your sentence structure and punctuation, as we shall see.) How do we define a motor car in order to delimit a boundary between it and other similar objects – a bus, a mini-bus? Is the vehicle sometimes known as a 'family wagon' a car? Is a station wagon or estate car a car? Criteria like the number of wheels or the size of engine are quickly eliminated as non-defining since they do not help us to delimit the boundary. We might then start to argue about the number of seats, the proportion of passenger space to luggage space within certain (to be defined) limits, or other more subtle criteria.

An old problem in linguistics concerns the definition of a word. Here is a popular or folk definition:

> A word is a sequence of letters which is separated from another by a space.

This definition has two fairly characteristic parts:

- The first clause assigns the phenomenon to be defined to a CLASS or CATEGORY of phenomena to which it belongs and which has other members – 'a sequence of letters'. (There will be other phenomena which are members of the class 'sequence of letters' but which are not words.)
- The 'which' clause assigns a defining CRITERION which distinguishes a word from the other possible members of the class. The criterion is the presence of a space that separates the sequences.

Now, were you to be writing on the adequacy of this defi-nition, you could look to the questions of whether it assigns a word to the right or the best class, and whether the defining criterion is adequate. The definition above assigns a word to a class of written or orthographic phenomena ('letters'). Against this, you might wish to argue that, irrespective of whether languages are written down, they all have words. Therefore a word is better assigned to the class of phonological phenomena (sounds). Moreover, the term 'sequence' is too vague, since any sequence is implied. The sequence of sounds must be STRUC-TURED (a new defining criterion) according to certain rules of word formation. These rules will become the substance of a new set of defining criteria to replace the one with which you began ('separated by a space'), a criterion that is no longer appropriate to a phonological phenomenon. This is the point at which your evolving definition will have to draw on the general kinds of criteria to be found in the discipline of linguistics: you would now have to become technical and to develop defining criteria by drawing on observations from phonetics and phonology, morphology (the forms of roots and inflexions in words), syntax (sentence structure) and semantics (meaning). Considerable space might need to be given to the elaboration of each of these issues. In this way a simple one-line definition grows into a major section of an essay or a whole essay itself.

The paragraphs below illustrate the beginnings of how this might be done. The first takes up the form of the definition and systematically builds upon the two major parts – the class membership statement and the ascription of defining characteristics. The second and third paragraphs introduce a discussion of the kinds of criteria that have been used. The suggestion by one linguist that a boundary be drawn around 'word' to distinguish it from a 'lexeme' is questioned, the more comprehensive definition being preferred.

> The popular definition of a word as 'a sequence of letters separated from another by a space' is deficient in many fundamental respects. In assuming that a word is an orthographical object, this definition neglects the primacy of sound in language: we speak of 'words' even in languages which have not been written down; and illiterate people who have never seen a page of print have no trouble identifying the words in their language.
>
> But this does not mean that a word can be defined as 'a sequence of sounds separated from another by a pause'. In the first place, the sequence must be a structured one, since all languages have phonological rules according to which sounds can be combined with one another. Secondly, the idea that there are 'pauses' between words in spoken language greatly

oversimplifies and misrepresents the phonetic facts. Finally, although a word is basically a phonological entity, it cannot be defined on criteria of sound alone. To define a word adequately it is necessary also to see it in three more ways: as a structured combination of morphological units; as an element in the syntactic structure of sentences (words form grammatical classes such as noun, verb and preposition); and as an element of language which carries meaning. Such a comprehensive approach results in this common definition: 'A word may be defined as the union of a particular meaning with a particular complex of sounds capable of a particular grammatical employment.'

By contrast, many attempts at defining the word have tended to concentrate on one or two of these criteria. Some linguists particularly exclude semantic properties of the word from its defining characteristics. Lyons (1968: 197–200), for example, defines a word purely grammatically, distinguishing it from a 'lexeme', which has properties of meaning. But there is, I believe, no good reason to exclude semantic or phonological criteria. A word is best viewed as a complex linguistic 'cluster concept', whose meaning can vary according to the context in which it is being used.

What we have here is not so much a definition as the opening to a discussion of what needs to be considered in order to arrive at a definition. Each of the points raised above would need to be elaborated in the ways you will now be familiar with. This discussion could conclude (though it might not have to, depending on the wording of the essay topic) with your own attempt at a definition.

You will have noticed that the discussion above introduces the question of whether a word should be distinguished in some fundamental way from a lexeme. Some essay topics will ask you quite explicitly to make such distinctions. As an example, here is a topic from anthropology:

> What is the difference between trade and exchange? Illustrate your answer with ethnographic examples.

The problem posed by a topic such as this is fundamentally the same as that we have just examined in connection with the word. You will, however, have to COMPARE the characteristics of each in order to arrive at a conclusion about which of them *best* distinguishes the one from the other. When you read the literature you will no doubt find that trade and exchange are not mutually exclusive terms but have certain overlapping characteristics in common – the non-defining characteristics. Alternatively, you might find that trade is a subclass of the more general class exchange (see the Euler circles in chapter 2, section 4.3). You might conclude that, although there is evidence that trade cannot be distinguished from exchange on simple economic grounds (both involve the fixing of the best price), exchange always involves certain distinguishing characteristics – a particular type of reciprocal obligation between groups, a particular type of ceremony, or something else. Your task will be to work out which of the various criteria suggested in your books best defines the difference and to separate from these the criteria which are not truly defining.

2.2 Defining and non-defining relative clauses

Ascribing defining and non-defining characteristics to phenomena is one of the most common actions you perform when writing, even when you are not consciously setting out to define a term or a concept. Almost every time you use an adjective before a noun you are raising the issue of whether that adjective assigns a defining or a non-defining characteristic to the phenomenon denoted by the noun. Look at this sentence:

> Freedman's recent book on Samoa aroused considerable
> controversy.

'Recent' is ambiguous. If this word represents a defining characteristic, then the statement implies that Freedman has written previous books on Samoa which were not controversial:

> Freedman's recent book on Samoa [unlike his earlier ones]
> aroused considerable controversy.

The phrase 'on Samoa', which comes after the noun, is similarly ambiguous. If 'recent' is interpreted to be defining in the sentence above, 'on Samoa' is non-defining. But what if Freedman has recently written books on other subjects?

> Freedman's recent book on Samoa [unlike his recent book on New Guinea] aroused considerable controversy.

'Recent' in this sentence is non-defining and 'on Samoa' is defining. Unless some clarifying phrase, like those between brackets in the sentences above, is added in, the only way to determine whether or not 'recent' and 'on Samoa' are defining is by looking up Freedman's publishing history. If the point you are making is at all important, you should save your reader this trouble by adding a clarifying comment.

Phrases like 'on Samoa' that come after the noun are sometimes called 'relatives'. Often, we write whole clauses that come after the noun, clauses which are typically introduced by 'who', 'whom', 'which' or 'that'. (This last sentence has two of them.) Like the relative phrase 'on Samoa', these clauses can be either defining or non-defining relatives (also known as 'restrictive' and 'non-restrictive' relatives). It is possible for you to indicate whether you intend your relative clause to ascribe a defining or a non-defining characteristic to the noun by two simple techniques.

The first lies in your choice of 'which' or 'that'. (With 'who' or 'whom' it is not possible to make this distinction.) If you want your relative clause to define the noun, it is usually possible to use either 'that' or 'which' to introduce it:

> The book that Freedman recently wrote about Samoa was very controversial.

> The book which Freedman recently wrote about Samoa was very controversial.

If, on the other hand, your relative clause is not intended to define the noun, you will not be able to use 'that'. In addition you must call on the second of the two distinguishing techniques, the comma:

> Freedman's book, *which* was about Samoa, was very controversial.

The 'which' clause bracketed by commas is an indication that the characteristic it ascribes to the book is not to be regarded as defining. The particular book in question will have been defined sufficiently by some preceding statement.

3 Comparing and contrasting

3.1 *The dynamics of comparison*

To compare and contrast is a very common requirement of the essay topics you are set. In addition, it is often necessary to engage in comparing and contrasting when you are dealing with topics worded in other ways. This kind of writing can be quite difficult to handle if you are unclear about the nature and purpose of comparison. The first thing to keep in mind is that it is fundamentally no different from the kind of analysis we have already learned about in this book. In particular, comparing and contrasting is hardly to be distinguished at all from defining.

If you ask yourself what the purpose of comparing two things could conceivably be, you will see that the answer can best be expressed in terms of defining the boundaries of one with respect to the other. For example, the topic we looked at above as an exercise in definition – 'What is the difference between trade and exchange?' – could equally have been worded 'Compare and contrast the notions of trade and exchange'. In order to carry out a comparison, we must therefore make use of those CRITERIA, about which we have had much to say in this chapter. We can only compare two things with respect to certain specified qualities or criteria. So the main difficulty in comparing and contrasting lies in finding them. It is this, rather than hunting about for 'similarities and differences', that you should concentrate on.

The shopping analogy we used earlier might help you see this. Compiling a list of the similarities and differences between brands does not of itself help you decide unless you order these characteristics according to some set of criteria – price, quality, durability, compatibility with what you already own, design, and so on. You must then WEIGHT or RANK these criteria according to some set of PRIORITIES you have established. Even if 'price is no object', some other criteria will be. You are also likely to find that each product has some features which are quite absent in the others. Listing these miscellaneous differences is of little help to your decision-making unless you have some means of assessing their importance. You cannot actually COMPARE or CONTRAST the quality of the four-speaker stereo-sound system fitted as standard in one motor car with that of the air-conditioning unit fitted to its competitor. All you can do is to rank these features with respect to what you think important in a car. That ranking will be affected by quite other criteria.

It is for these reasons that listing a set of descriptive characteristics on one side of a page and another set for the contrasting phenomenon on the other side is by itself insufficient as a method of preparing your comparative essay. Let us take a topic from sociology:

> Compare the functionalist and Marxist perspectives on the institution of the family.

One common way of preparing an essay on a topic like this is to make a heading 'Functionalist perspectives' and another 'Marxist perspectives' and then list the perspectives under each heading. But a better way might be first to work out which institutional features of the family need to be explained, for example its status as an economic unit, its function as an institution to care for and to socialise children, its position as a microcosm of the gender and political hierarchy in society, its role in reproducing the attitudes and beliefs of a society. Having worked these out, you can then set down the functionalist and Marxist approaches to each one. You should then be in a position to decide on which criterion or set of criteria fundamentally unifies or separates (as the case may be) these two perspectives on the family.

In the attempt at an opening to an essay on this topic below, the defining criteria suggested are inequality, exploitation, conflict versus consensus and change versus stability:

Marxists and functionalists both view the traditional family as a key unit of industrial capitalism, which it helps to maintain and reproduce. In drawing attention to the essentially exploitative nature of the relation between capital and labour, Marxists emphasise the conflict between them. Out of this conflict will come change. Functionalists, on the other hand, stress the mechanisms by which consensus and stability in society are attained, even in the face of inequality and a certain degree of exploitation (or alienation). For the functionalist society is first and foremost a system. Although there will be tensions and even contradictions in this system, all its parts are constantly being modified in order to preserve the essential stability of the system as a whole. These fundamental differences of viewpoint about society are reproduced in the Marxist and functionalist analyses of the family.

To the Marxist the internal structure of the family as an economic unit reflects the division of labour and the domination of labour by capital to be found in the economy as a whole. And, like the worker in a factory, the family unit is exploited by the requirements of capitalistic production. The family also serves to perpetuate the class divisions of society through the inheritance of property. The functionalist, by contrast, sees the division of labour and economic power as a necessary adjustment to economic reality and social stability, and argues that the distribution of economic power both in the family itself and the society as a whole is much more fluid than the Marxist admits. Because the notions of inequality and exploitation are found in both theories, they do not clearly distinguish them. For the functionalist, inequality and the exploitation of the family by capital is not complete, and is offset by other economic benefits which began to accrue when production moved out of the home. The Marxist emphasises the way in which the multiplication of small family units offers an enormous captive market for the products of capitalist manufacturing.

The family is, however, more than an economic unit of society. Similar differences between Marxists and functionalists can be seen in other facets of the family institution: the socialisation of children, the gender and other distributions of political power, and the reproduction of social and cultural values. As we examine each in turn we shall see how the differences between Marxists and functionalists on inequality and exploitation are really differences of degree. Their perspectives on conflict and consensus and on change and stability in the family are, by contrast, quite different in kind.

You will see that this piece of writing is organised on the basis of the defining criteria (inequality, exploitation, conflict, etc.) and the characteristics of the family itself. Doing it this way means that one is continually moving back and forth between what the two perspectives have to say with respect to these things. This movement is signalled by such words and phrases as 'by contrast', 'on the other hand' and 'more . . . than'.

Now, this is not the only way to organise a comparative piece. It is certainly possible to set up the essay as a whole in this fashion:

1. *Marxist perspectives*
   Economic issues
   Socialisation of children
   Gender distribution of power
   Other aspects of power distribution
   Reproduction of social and cultural values

2. *Functionalist perspectives*
   Economic issues
   Socialisation of children
   Gender distribution of political power
   Other aspects of power distribution
   Reproduction of social and cultural values

3. *Conclusion (synthesis)*

This traditional schema for a comparative essay is still to be found and can be made to work quite well. But unless you can operate it with skill, it does have certain dangers. You are very likely to be tempted into writing two 'mini-essays' (one on each perspective) rather than a well-integrated comparison. If this does happen, it is almost impossible to write a conclusion which effectively synthesises the critical issues. What tends to get lost is that fundamental constituent of any good essay, the case for which you are arguing. In addition, you will see such a schema makes it easier to shirk the hunt for the defining criteria on which your comparative analysis should be based.

In sum, approach an essay or part of an essay which demands comparison in the same analytical spirit which you will devote to any other kind of writing. As you expand on the fundamental points you want to make, you will find that not only a sentence or two but a whole paragraph or a series of paragraphs will be needed to explain one of the phenomena to be compared. The special demand of comparison is that for each of these paragraphs an answering one is required to take up the very same issues. This continuous antiphonal structure, in which the one explanation is immediately answered by the other, is the best means of ensuring that everything you say remains relevant to the question and advances the argument.

3.2 *Comparative structures*

Comparing and contrasting can only be carried out on what we perceive to be like phenomena. You cannot compare the population distribution of hunters and gatherers in Namibia with the colour of the paint on your bedroom walls unless, by some feat of ingenuity, you can find some quality in common between the two. There needs always, as we have just seen, to be an 'answering' – a parallelism – between the two or more things to be compared.

This means that when you structure your sentences you must

take special care that you do compare like with like. You cannot, for example, compare Marxism with functionalists, because one is a doctrine or theory and the other a group of people:

> Marxism emphasises change whereas functionalists stress the grounds of social stability.

You need to decide for each sentence whether to write about the theory or about the adherents of the theory:

> Marxism emphasises change whereas functionalism stresses the grounds of social stability.

or:

> Marxists emphasise change whereas functionalists stress the grounds of social stability.

When writing comparative statements always check them out to ensure that this parallelism is maintained. One of the most common mistakes of this kind is to compare two incompatible objects:

> Marx's arguments lose nothing in comparison with his detractors.

Marx can be compared with his detractors, or his arguments with his detractors' arguments. Hence you might write:

> Marx's arguments lose nothing when compared with those of his detractors.

or:

> Marx's arguments lose nothing when compared with his detractors'.

Similarly, take care that you do not compare an action with an object:

> Marx in his early works placed great emphasis on the concept of alienation, like Weber.

Rather, you might write:

> Marx in his early works placed great emphasis on the concept of alienation, as did Weber.

We cannot exemplify all the unhappy combinations of people, objects, actions, activities, situations, states and relations that are easily miscompared. Since it is very easy to confuse these things when you first set down a comparative structure, take care to check them as you write. You will remember from chapter 8 (p. 185) that falling between two stools is a common cause of injuries to sentences. Since comparison, by its very nature, demands a parallelism between like and like, your sentence structure needs to reflect this.

A final word about the preposition to use with 'compare'. When Shakespeare wrote in Sonnet 18 'Shall I compare thee to a summer's day?', he was assuming that the summer's day is a conventional standard or criterion *to* which his loved one was superior. Most of your academic writing is not like this. You will be comparing the qualities of one thing *with* those of another, weighing them as in a scale. You might make a summary judgement in a situation where Marx is being set up as the conventional standard:

> Compared *to* Marx, Weber made a more subtle and lasting contribution to the understanding of society.

Where, on the other hand, you are being asked to weigh the relative merits of Marx and Weber according to criteria you yourself have to establish in your essay, you will be comparing Marx *with* Weber. To compare one thing to another is to accept a conventional criterion; to compare one with another is to question and discuss the very criteria on which your judgement is to be made. This latter is one of the fundamental demands of good academic writing.

10
Cohesion and texture

> ... to combine textural appeal with an
> appropriate scheme of textual
> cohesion, in such a way that one
> supports the other, is a fundamental
> stylistic task. The text, however, has
> primacy; plot is more important than
> diction, though diction may be
> involved in plot.
>
> WALTER NASH

1 Determinants of cohesion and texture

A coherent essay depends in the first instance, as we have seen in
many preceding chapters, on the careful formulation of the case
to be argued. If your answer to the question posed is conceived
as a 'golden thread' that runs right through the piece of writing,
it is in the answer itself and its various implications that the
beginnings of coherence lie. But once you have decided on your
answer, you cannot assume that there is some natural order of
thought that produces in your essay a coherence that is above
and beyond the details of the words you use. It is in your
disposition of grammatical structures and in your choice and
deployment of those words that you bring your text together. To
work at this is to produce COHESION and TEXTURE in your
writing.

Text consists in your attempts to bring all the elements of your
writing together into a unified whole. The language makes
provision for this, such that the connections between words and
between structures can be made more or less explicit to your
readers in various ways and to varying degrees. The rudiments of
this process we have already examined. In this chapter we shall
look much more closely at the ways in which the details of your
language can make the difference between a text which satisfies
the minimal requirements of coherence and one which does its

best to draw as many of its elements as you can manage into that unified whole.

These features of cohesion and texture are not superficial. Although some of them play about the surfaces of words and structures – reflecting, refracting and intensifying relationships of meaning – together they give an added depth to what you have to write. To attend to these things in your writing is not to seek after a 'style' quite separate from your thought. To do so is rather to use the resources of the language to find out for yourself what the main streams of your thought really are. (This is why, in order to emphasise the contrast between the ideas of the last two sentences, not only did I need the sentence link 'rather', I had to ensure that both sentences started with the same infinitive structure 'To ...'.) Certainly, much of this operates in the subconscious both of the writer and the reader. If, by attending consciously to some of the techniques of writing set out in this chapter you can make them part of yourself, your tutor will be grateful – even if he or she cannot say exactly why.

Although, as we have said, some of your textual effects will be subconscious, it is in the conscious revision of your text that you will be able to rework some of its major deficiencies into a better unified whole. (This is one reason for leaving sufficient time for revision.) The main things you need to attend to in this revision are these: sentence adverbials, referring expressions, coordinating structures and vocabulary.

1.1 Sentence adverbials (linking terms)

Signal to yourself and your reader where you are going and what you are DOING. Most of the signals you need to send have been covered in chapters 3, 5 and 8. The basic sets of signals are the sentence adverbials and other linking terms (e.g. firstly, furthermore, in particular, consequently, in other words, alternatively, in comparison, by contrast, similarly, admittedly, certainly, to digress, to recapitulate, to resume). These are the terms in which you point out just how you are extending, elaborating, enhanc-

ing or analysing your material and structuring your own text.
About these we shall say no more.

1.2 *Referring expressions*

Referring expressions are used to help clarify what goes with
what in your text. A subject or participant introduced at one
point in the text becomes the fulcrum on which both earlier and
later references to it will turn. Referring expressions include:

- the definite article 'the';
- the pronouns 'it', 'he', 'she', 'they', 'him', 'her', 'them';
- the demonstratives 'this', 'that', 'these', 'those';
- the quantifiers 'some', 'many', 'much', 'all', 'none', 'each', 'any',
  etc.
- other terms: 'such', 'so', 'the very . . .', 'the same . . .',
  'previously', 'the former', 'the latter' (note the double 't' in the
  spelling of this word), 'here' and (at a more distant remove in
  your text) 'there', 'earlier' and 'above'.

All these words refer *backwards* in your text to participants you
have announced earlier. What you must take pains to ensure is
that the *particular* word, phrase or statement to which they refer
is crystal clear. Confusion sets in if your reader cannot work out
quickly and precisely what an 'it', a 'this' or an 'each' refers to. If
there is doubt, it is better to repeat the word or phrase itself.

Similarly, there are words and phrases which refer *forwards* in
your text (e.g. below, as we shall see, thus, the following, to be
discussed). In addition, the colon (:) is a punctuation mark that
refers forwards.

1.3 *Coordinating structures*

When you are building up stretches of text, cast your eye back to
see whether you have used your grammatical structures to
achieve cohesion. Constructing a piece of writing has much in
common with constructing anything else. The parts to be joined

together – in this case grammatical structures – have to be sufficiently alike in shape at the place where they meet to fit securely. A nut and a bolt are quite different objects; but their threads need to match.

Two very common structures can be troublesome. With number it is quite easy to slip inadvertently from singular to plural; and with tense present and past are easily pushed into an unhappy union. (We noticed a slip of tense in the passage by Sabine on Edmund Burke's conception of natural rights, on p. 151 above.) If you do find yourself switching number or tense about too often, this lack of cohesion might have quite deep-seated causes. These causes are examined in chapter 7, section 2.3, and chapter 8, section 3.4.

Coordination is typically performed by 'and', 'in addition', 'or', 'but' and their equivalents, as well as by other devices. When you bring two ideas together in this way, check that the two structures on either side of the join are parallel. The first sentence of this paragraph is a case in point. Two sets of terms are coordinated by 'as well as'. Both these sets of terms are dominated by the word 'performed'. In order to secure the join, the 'by' in the first set is repeated in the second. Now, it is perfectly acceptable in short simple coordinations to omit the second of these binding elements:

> Coordination is typically performed by coordinate
> conjunctions, (by) certain adverbials and (by) other devices.

But academic prose is in part characterised by the complexity of the elements to be coordinated – in sentences, in paragraphs and over a whole essay. It therefore becomes extremely important to develop a consistency of structure and to draw attention to that consistency by preserving the structural parallels and repeating the motifs that make them apparent. The architecture of prose is in this respect similar to that of a building or a piece of music.

In order to give you some idea of what can happen when structural coordination is neglected, I shall rewrite the three sentences immediately above in an uncoordinated way. Un-parallel forms are italicised and omissions indicated with a caret:

> But academic prose is in part characterised by the complexity of elements to be coordinated – in sentences, ∧ paragraphs and ∧ a whole essay. It therefore becomes extremely important to develop a consistency of structure and *drawing* attention to that consistency by preserving the structural parallels and *repeat* the motifs that make them apparent. The architecture of prose is in this respect similar to ∧ a building or ∧ piece of music.

One situation in which you should always check the consistency of your structures is when you are making a list. Here is a list in which the items are not parallel:

> There are four features of cohesion to be attended to virtually simultaneously:
> – sentence adverbials;
> – ensuring that referring expressions do in fact refer to the terms intended;
> – keep your coordinate structures grammatically parallel;
> – vocabulary should be chosen with an eye to other words used in the text.

Not one of the items in this list is parallel with another. In sorting out which structure to use and repeat, go back to your introductory statement and decide what your wording demands. In the present case the list is to be of 'features to be attended to', so each must include a feature of cohesion and the kind of attention it needs:

> There are four features of cohesion to be attended to virtually simultaneously:
> – sentence adverbials need to be carefully distributed;
> – referring expressions must be made to refer to the terms intended;
> – coordinated structures should be kept parallel;

- vocabulary should be chosen with an eye to other words in the text.

1.4 *Vocabulary*

A careful patterning of your vocabulary is one of the things which brings most satisfaction in the act of writing and, by greatly enhancing the texture of your prose, makes it satisfying to read. This kind of patterning – lexical cohesion – can be achieved in many different ways. We shall touch here on just two – repetition and substitution.

Whether you repeat a word or substitute a synonym for it cannot easily be considered separately, since a decision to repeat a word will be affected in part by what substitutes might be used. Inexperienced writers tend to repeat a key word either far too much or hardly at all. You might remember the kind of story you wrote as a child:

> The dog bit the man. Then the dog ran into the barn. The man chased the dog into the barn and the dog bit the man again.

> The dog bit the man. Then he ran into the barn and he chased him and he bit him again.

Other writers go to extraordinary lengths to avoid repetition, with comical results:

> The dog bit the man. Then the canine ran into the barn, where he was chased by the unfortunate victim. But the cur again sank his fangs into the now doubly abused personage.

The art of achieving lexical cohesion is to decide which words are the important ones in the thematic structure of your text and to drop them into the argument as a recurring motif – not so heavily as to make your reader think you have a very limited vocabulary, nor so lightly as to have them go quite unremarked. In *The Tempest* Shakespeare performs intricate thematic arabesques with 'Art', 'power', 'master', 'slave', 'dream', 'spirit', 'music', 'freedom', 'air', 'earth', 'sea', 'Nature' and other words which underlie the 'argument' of the play. An academic essay does not, of course, attempt the complexity of lexical patterning to be found in much literature for the reason that the former's argument tends to be more restricted in scope. Nevertheless, your prose will be much less cohesive – and your thought correspondingly less coherent – if you always choose a word in virtual isolation from the others on your page.

We shall now examine lexical cohesion as well as the other kinds of cohesion set out above in an extended example.

2 Revising and improving text

Here is a topic on Shakespeare's play *The Tempest*:

> 'Learning is a major theme in the play; we learn that Miranda is capable of it and Caliban not, and why this should be so; but [in Prospero] we are also given a plan of the place of learning in the dispositions of providence.' (Frank Kermode)

> Discuss learning and knowledge as it is portrayed in *The Tempest*.

First, I shall present an opening paragraph stripped of as many features of cohesion and texture as is possible without producing something entirely unintelligible. Then I shall set out the paragraph as it was first drafted and add a few more paragraphs to it to develop some parts of the argument. This is a moderately cohesive piece of writing. But it is capable of much improvement. The improved version is then presented.

> 1
>
> In *The Tempest* reason is set against 'fury', nurture nature. The duke is not the perfect expression of the providential power of knowledge and civilisation. Caliban is not ruled solely by passion and unregenerate nature. Prospero's Art is not a humane kind of learning and the duke renounces magic at the end of the play. Caliban is not what he says – 'A devil, a born

devil, on whose nature / Nurture can never stick.' Caliban does learn. At the end of the play Caliban says 'I'll be wise hereafter, / And seek for grace.' Prospero does not. If we are to look for a criterion of knowledge it will be Miranda, in whom there is nature, reason, nurture and passion. Miranda does not know very much about the world. On seeing Ferdinand Miranda says, without any hint of metaphor, that Ferdinand is a spirit, 'a thing divine'. What she displays is more important.

Did you work out the connections between reason, fury, nature, nurture, Art, magic, passion and civilisation? What is the relation between the duke and Prospero? What is the relation between Prospero, Caliban and Miranda? Who said that Caliban is 'a devil, a born devil'? What doesn't Prospero do? How can Miranda be a criterion of knowledge if she does not know much about the world? What is it she displays that is more important than what?

If you know *The Tempest* you might be able to draw on your knowledge to answer many of these questions without too much difficulty. If you do not, you will have to hunt around in this first text fairly assiduously before clues to some of the answers become apparent. The next (extended) version should make most, but not all, of these questions much easier to answer.

2

In *The Tempest* reason is set against 'fury' and nurture against nature. But the duke Prospero is not the perfect exemplar of the providential power of reason and nurture any more than Caliban is a savage ruled solely by fury and unregenerate nature. Prospero's magical Art, despite the contrast he draws with the magic of 'the foul witch Sycorax', is not a humane kind of learning; for otherwise he would have no cause to renounce it at the end of the play. Nor is it true, as Prospero says of Caliban, that he is 'A devil, a born devil, on whose nature / Nurture can never stick.' Caliban does learn, arguably even more than Prospero, inasmuch as at the end of the play he says 'I'll be wise hereafter, / And seek for grace', which finds no echo in anything Prospero says. If we are to look for a

touchstone to knowledge in *The Tempest*, it will be found in
Miranda, in whom nature and nurture, reason and passion are
perfectly mixed. Miranda does not 'know' very much at all
about the world: on first seeing Ferdinand she thinks him,
without any hint of metaphor, a spirit, 'a thing divine'. What
she displays is something more important, a depth of
understanding or sympathy.

Prospero's learning seems to be of two quite distinct kinds.
Neither is admirable. In recounting the story of how he was
dispossessed of his dukedom, he boasts to Miranda how

>   being so reputed
> In dignity, and for the liberal Arts
> Without a parallel; those being all my study,
> The government I cast upon my brother,
> And to my state grew stranger, being transported
> And rapt in secret studies.   (I, ii, 72–7)

Prospero's studies were of the seven traditional liberal arts, and
through absorption in them forfeited his power in the state. A
duke cannot be a pure scholar or theoretician. These liberal
studies were not the magical Art that he practised on the island
(the studies were 'secret' only in the sense that they were
private and recondite). This latter 'so potent Art' was studied
solely for the power it bestowes on an egocentric Prospero to
do violence to nature ('I have bedimm'd / The noontide sun')
and to effect his revenge on other people. We notice that the
volumes that Prospero prizes 'above my dukedom' become a
single book (III, i, 94; V, i, 57), which he consults to further his
project and which he promises to drown only when he can be
sure that he will no longer have to rely on it. The book to
Prospero is little more than the bottle to the drunken butler
Stephano.

This is something Caliban learns. He knows better than
Stephano and Trinculo that the rebellion against Prospero can
only succeed if first they burn his books; for without them
Prospero is 'but a sot, as I am, nor hath not / One spirit to
command'. There is a clear parallel between the effect of
Stephano's 'celestial liquor' on Caliban and Prospero's charms
– 'the ignorant fumes that mantle / Their clearer reason' – on

the usurpers he wishes to subdue. The sense of power conferred by the butt of sack is, of course, illusory; but so is that of Prospero's Art. Both turn ordinary mortals into 'masters' (a word used constantly throughout the play). But true learning is not a matter of attaining mastery over nature, over other people or even, through the use of reason, over oneself. This is the point which Gonzalo wishes to have set down 'With gold on lasting pillars':

> in one voyage
> Did Claribel her husband find at Tunis,
> And Ferdinand, her brother, found a wife
> Where he himself was lost, Prospero his dukedom
> In a poor isle, and all of us ourselves
> When no man was his own.   (V, i, 208–13)

Some of the answers to the questions raised with respect to (1) should now be much easier to see. It should be clear that reason and nurture are being contrasted with 'fury' and nature, and that Prospero (who is himself the duke) is not a perfect specimen of good learning any more than Caliban completely represents its absence. This draft does not, however, make it clear early on that Caliban is Prospero's slave or that Miranda is Prospero's daughter. We now know that it is Prospero who calls Caliban 'A devil, a born devil', and that the master suffers by comparison with his slave in that he does not learn enough by the end of the play to ask for grace. With respect to Miranda, it is made clearer that 'knowing' about the world is less important than another kind of learning with which this is contrasted – understanding or sympathy.

The first paragraph is built on a series of contrasts. For the most part the devices of cohesion have been sufficiently employed to clarify the main lines of these contrasts. Linking terms are there, referring expressions do their job and the contrasts are pointed up by the coordination devices of the grammar. There are a few slips on some of these counts, both in this paragraph and the two that follow: 'the' in line 2 and an omitted 'he' before 'forfeited' in line 11 of the second paragraph are two of them. But what is perhaps principally lacking is the extra dimension of cohesion produced by vocabulary. True, 'reason', 'fury', 'nature' and ' nurture' are repeated throughout. 'Expression' (line 2) and 'criterion' (line 14) are changed to 'exemplar' and 'touchstone' – modifications which might point the contrast between Prospero and Miranda a little bit better, but which are still rather lame. 'Art' is left hanging until the second paragraph. By and large this draft is pretty thin soup.

The finished text, (3) below, attempts to clean up the mistakes, repair the omissions and to point up the main themes of the argument. The chief thrust of these changes is to establish more securely the theme of mastery in learning and the connections it has with an illusory sense of power over nature and other people. Hence Prospero's schoolmastering is introduced in the second paragraph as a preparation for the argument that follows. The experimental, alchemical nature of Prospero's art is given more emphasis ('philosopher's stone' is implicitly contrasted with 'touchstone'); and the distinction between the conventional 'studies' of volumes in the liberal arts, which led to his loss of power, and the use of his 'book' as an experimental manual or handbook to regain power is made clearer. The difference between Prospero's view of knowledge as reason and the alternative view of it as understanding and sympathy is reinforced in the last sentence of the passage by the substitution of 'insight' for 'point'. ('Cool' is added in line 13 of the last paragraph to allude to some lines in *A Midsummer Night's Dream* in which Theseus asserts the limitations of reason.) There are other lexical changes too. In the first paragraph there is a stress on white, enlightened, civilised; and black, dark, ignorant, savage. The contrast between what Caliban and Prospero 'say' becomes more sharply focused in that the one 'resolves' and the other 'promises'.

There are many other changes, all designed to improve cohesion and texture, for example the adding in of new sentences to open and close the first paragraph. If you wish to plot all these changes in detail, you will find the annotated manuscript of (2) reproduced in Appendix 3.

3

In *The Tempest* Shakespeare takes up common Elizabethan and Jacobean themes of learning. Reason is set against 'fury' and nurture against nature. But these themes are not resolved by the simple triumph of reason and nurture on the one hand over nature and 'fury' (or passion) on the other. Prospero, the exiled Duke of Milan, though the dominant force in the play, is not a perfect exemplar of the providential power of reason and nurture, any more than his slave Caliban is a savage ruled solely by fury and unregenerate nature. Prospero's white magical Art, despite the contrasts he himself draws with the black magic of 'the foul witch Sycorax', is not a humane kind of learning; for otherwise he would have no cause to renounce it at the end of the play. His Art is alchemical and redolent of the philosopher's stone. Nor is it true, as Prospero says of Caliban, that the slave is 'A devil, a born devil, on whose nature / Nurture can never stick' (IV, i, 188–9). Caliban does learn, arguably even more than Prospero, inasmuch as at the end of the play he resolves 'I'll be wise hereafter, / And seek for grace.' This is a resolution which finds no echo in anything Prospero promises. Prospero is not a white, enlightened master of civilisation; Caliban is not a dark, ignorant slave of nature. Shakespeare in this play is testing and revising the conventional dichotomies of his time.

If we are to look for a touchstone to knowledge in *The Tempest*, it will be found in Prospero's daughter Miranda, in whom nature and nurture, reason and passion are perfectly mixed. Miranda's rather special kind of knowledge is not the product of Prospero's own irascible and peremptory schoolmastering: 'Dost thou attend me? . . . Thou attend'st me not . . . Dost thou hear?' (I, ii, 78ff). Miranda is always acquiescent in this didactic tutoring. But at the end of it all, she does not actually 'know' very much about the world. On first seeing the prince Ferdinand she thinks him, without any hint of metaphor, a spirit, 'a thing divine'. The kind of learning she does display is a quality vastly more important than anything her father has actually taught her – a depth of human understanding or sympathy.

Prospero's learning seems to be of two quite distinct kinds. Neither proves to be admirable. In recounting the story of how he was dispossessed of his dukedom, he boasts to Miranda how

> being so reputed
> In dignity, and for the liberal Arts
> Without a parallel; those being all my study,
> The government I cast upon my brother,
> And to my state grew stranger, being transported
> And rapt in secret studies.   (I, ii, 72–7)

Prospero's studies were in the seven conventional liberal arts, and through absorption in them he forfeited his power in the state. A duke, he now realises, cannot be a pure scholar or theoretician. The studies were 'secret' only in the sense that they were private and recondite. These liberal arts he then replaces with the less conventional magical Art that he practises on the island. This latter is a 'so potent Art' that he makes use of solely for the power it bestows on an egocentric Prospero to do violence to nature ('I have bedimm'd / The noontide sun . . . Set roaring war: to the dread rattling thunder / Have I given fire' (V, i, 41ff). Learning of this kind is effected solely for revenge on those who toppled him from his dukedom. We notice, too, that the volumes that he once prized 'above my dukedom' have become whittled down to a single 'book' (III, i, 94; V, i, 57), which Prospero consults as a manual to further his experimental project with nature and human beings. This handbook he promises to drown only when he can be sure that he will no longer have to rely on it. Prospero's book is Stephano's bottle.

This is something Caliban learns. He knows better than the drunken butler Stephano and the equally drunken jester Trinculo that the rebellion all three hatch against Prospero to dispossess him of the island can only succeed if first they burn the master's books. Without them, Caliban has realised, Prospero is 'but a sot, as I am, nor hath not / One spirit to command' (III, ii, 90–1). Caliban also learns by the end of the play that he was a 'thrice-double ass . . . to take this drunkard for a god' (V, i, 295–6). Shakespeare draws a clear parallel between the effect of Stephano's 'celestial liquor' on Caliban and the effect of Prospero's charms – 'the ignorant fumes that mantle / Their clearer reason' (V, i, 67–8) – on the usurpers the duke wishes to master. The sense of power conferred by the butt of sack is, of course, illusory; but so is that of Prospero's Art. Both turn ordinary mortals into 'masters', a word used constantly throughout the play to suggest at once authority and lack of control.

True learning is not a matter of attaining mastery over nature, over other people or even, through the use of cool reason, over oneself. True learning is the kind of understanding which comes not from any 'master' in the play but from the young Miranda and the old Counsellor Gonzalo. It is Gonzalo who wishes this insight to be set down 'With gold on lasting pillars':

> in one voyage
> Did Claribel her husband find at Tunis,
> And Ferdinand, her brother, found a wife
> Where he himself was lost, Prospero his dukedom
> In a poor isle, and all of us ourselves
> When no man was his own.   (V, i, 208–13)

11
Conventions of academic writing

1 Academic culture

To be a student in a college or a university is not only to be a learner. It is also to be a member of a community and a culture with customs, myths and rituals which differentiate it in significant ways from other communities and cultures to which you might belong – sporting clubs, churches, political parties, and so on. To be in university or college is to submit to a sometimes bewildering array of customs and expectations that can take many, many months to feel at home with. To study history or anthropology is to enter the department of history or the department of anthropology, where you are quite likely to be regarded as having begun a novitiate to the vocation of historian or anthropologist. You must therefore learn the customs and rituals of the vocation.

Most departments initiate you by providing a manual or outline of studies for the year. In this there will often be a section called 'Essay writing' or, more candidly, 'Rules for the presentation of written work'. These are the rules you have to learn, notwithstanding the initially confusing fact that the requirements of one department might well conflict with those of another. A book like the present one can therefore give you no more than a very general overview of the matters you need to attend to, and can merely draw your attention to what to look for when you study the departmental rules. If these rules fail to give you direction on any matter, you might need to consult one of the many style manuals available. Always, in such circumstances, try to get hold of a manual specific to the discipline in which you are writing. Where you cannot be quite sure which convention to adopt, choose one you think is likely to be satisfactory and try to be CONSISTENT in your use of it.

These rules are conventional, but that does not necessarily make them wholly arbitrary. Some, it is true, have simply become fossilised in particular disciplines, for example the Latinisms *supra* and *infra* ('above' and 'below') of certain footnoting systems. Others, by contrast, have grown out of the need to solve particular problems of method and technique in the analysis of certain kinds of primary evidence. For example, the Harvard referencing system – in which a source is specified in the text by author's name, date of publication and page number (Smith 1984: 263) – might be quite adequate for most writing in the social sciences but useless to the historian or literary scholar. Other conventions of style, particularly with respect to punctuation, are adopted for typographical reasons: certain things are thought by some to look better on a page of print, for example NATO, BBC, NSW rather than N.A.T.O., B.B.C., N.S.W. There will often be other justifications for a convention. Your immediate task is less to worry about these justifications than to find out (sometimes by trial and error) which of these rules are quite rigidly enforced in a given department and which not.

2 A skeleton key to stylistic conventions

2.1 Formal and informal language

Academic language need not be stuffy. Even so, the colloquialisms of conversation and the informalities of advertising copy and of certain newspapers and magazines are best avoided. Good language thrives on variety and freshness, but what is fresh and acceptable in one context might be simply gauche in another.

Conventions of academic writing

Here are a few pointers which are fairly reliable in all your academic writing.

Contracted speech forms

Contractions like 'don't', 'didn't', 'haven't', 'I'll', 'she's' and 'they're' should be kept for talking about your work with your tutor or friends. (I have used them in this book, which is less formal than an essay.)

You, we, I

Unlike a guide such as this, an academic essay does not directly address the tutor. 'You' should be kept out of an essay. Use it for a seminar, a tutorial delivery or a conversation with friends and tutors. 'We' will usually do as a substitute for the colloquial 'you'. On the uses of 'I' and 'we', see the discussion on pp. 143–6.

Which, because, whereas

These might be effective in some contexts to introduce a free-standing sentence with a single main proposition:

> Tennyson College provides the best apiculture courses and computer facilities in this part of the nation. Which is one reason why studying in this humming hub of academe will give you a buzz.

An academic essay is not the appropriate place for this kind of structure. On 'because' and 'whereas', see p. 168.

Abbreviations

Practice with abbreviations varies considerably. Even common ones, like e.g., Unesco or MP, should be approached warily. Some disciplines, departments or individual lecturers will always prefer 'for example' to the abbreviation. Well-known acronyms like Unesco or Anzac, which have passed into the language, are usually acceptable. With a less well known one (judgement on this will often depend on which part of the world you live in), the best procedure is to write the name out in full at first mention and include the abbreviation in parentheses (e.g. South East Asia Treaty Organisation (SEATO)). Thereafter, you can use the abbreviation alone. This rule is sometimes applied to standard technical abbreviations (e.g. kilometres (km.)) where much use has to be made of it. 'Etc.' is probably best avoided altogether, and is not improved by writing 'etcetera'. Prefer 'and so on', but use it sparingly.

2.2 Technical vocabulary

The very particular technical vocabularies appropriate to some disciplines may not travel well to others. This is sometimes because the concept is simply inappropriate to the modes of analysis in the other disciplines. Sometimes the reason is ideological or political. (The practitioners of one discipline often dislike their language being colonised by the vocabulary of another.) While you might write with impunity about 'the socialisation of the child' in any department of sociology, you must consider carefully whether to write of 'the socialisation of Jane Eyre' in an essay on Brontë's novel for your English department. If you suspect that a word or phrase has a loaded meaning in one department, or for some school of thought, test the waters in other departments before you throw it in. One way of doing this is to listen carefully to the words your lecturers use, and to drop any doubtful word into a tutorial discussion to see how it is received.

2.3 Layout

Layout concerns the disposition of your text on the page. Every reader appreciates a well-designed page, which does much to compensate even for indifferent handwriting. Pay attention to rules like the confining of your text to one side of the paper, the numbering of pages and the width of margins. Bear in mind that you want the tutor marking your essay to start out well-disposed towards the job of reading what you have written.

Headings and subheadings

In some departments and disciplines you will be commended for laying out your essay with numbered sections, headings and subheadings. It is sometimes done in the manner of this book; at other times a mixture of Roman numerals, Arabic numerals and letters is preferred. Some departments encourage you to use numbered subheadings for reports or field studies but not for essays. In yet others the merest sign of a numbered paragraph, a subheading or even a list of numbered points (i) ... (ii) ... (iii) within your text will be to offend certain traditions and sensibilities. Generally speaking, the younger the discipline and the more closely oriented to the social sciences the more disposed it is to use these devices of layout. Do not, even so, use them as a substitute for developing a coherent argument throughout the essay. Excessive use of numbered subheadings will often clearly betray a scissors-and-paste piece of work.

Tables and figures

Tables and figures are a useful way of summarising information in a manner clearer and more succinct than ordinary prose. ('Figure' is the name given to any diagram or illustration other than a table or a photograph, which is called a 'plate'.) They should always be positioned as closely as possible to your discussion of them in the text, and you must always ensure that you do discuss them rather than let them 'speak for themselves'. Normally tables and figures are numbered consecutively throughout the essay and referred to in your text as Table 1, Table 2, etc. and Figure 1, Figure 2, etc. Each table or figure should have, together with its number, a caption explaining what it is. Tables commonly have their numbers and captions positioned above, while figures have theirs below.

The ability to construct good tables and figures is an important skill to acquire if you are working in the social sciences. Books on methodology in the social sciences and manuals of scientific writing are the best sources of advice.

Indenting of paragraphs

Unless your matter is a long quotation or something else inset into the text, indent the first line of each paragraph. If you do not, it can be difficult for a reader to see where a new paragraph begins if the preceding one finishes at the end of a line. One way of overcoming this is to leave double your usual space between paragraphs. Indenting, however, is the more widespread practice.

2.4 Quotations

The setting-out of quotations often causes difficulty. The common conventions are these:

- If your quotation will take up more than three or four lines of your page (some style guides allow as much as 100 words), indent the whole quotation, keeping the left margin straight. An indented quotation does not need to be enclosed by quotation marks.
- If your quotation is shorter than this, you can incorporate it into your text. (Essays on poetry might occasionally prefer to indent even a one-line quotation.) In this case you must use quotation marks. The rules of whether to use single quotation marks (') or double (") may vary. Check your style guide. If you are in doubt use single quotation marks.
- If you leave out any words in the quotation, mark this ellipsis with three dots.
- You may modify the original structure of words or insert words of your own into a quotation. You will often need to do this in order to preserve the grammatical structure of your own sentence, into which the quotation is integrated. Interpolations are also used to clarify something the quoted material leaves vague, for example by substituting a name for 'he' or 'she'. Any such modification of the author's words must be signalled by enclosing the interpolations in *square* brackets. For example, Sabine asserts: 'It is true that [Burke] never denied the reality of natural rights.'

2.5 *Notes*

Notes may be placed either at the bottom of the page (footnotes) or at the end of the essay (endnotes). They may be numbered consecutively throughout the essay or from 1 on each page. Some disciplines have strict conventions governing either or both of these. Study your style guide. There are also conventions governing where you place the identifying number in your text. The most common in the arts disciplines is to place it at the end of the appropriate sentence or after the nearest punctuation mark after your reference. You may, however, be permitted to place it somewhere else within the sentence.

2.6 *References and bibliographies*

The permutations and combinations of the elements of order, punctuation and other things in references and bibliographies are almost endless. When you are doing your references, put your style guide in front of you and follow it not only to the letter but to the very comma.

The structural bones of a reference are these:

- author's family name;
- author's initials or given name;
- the title of the article (where appropriate);
- the title of the book or the name of the journal;
- the volume number;
- the place of publication (usually the name of the town or the city is enough; small towns will often be complemented by the name of the county or state);
- the name of the publisher;
- the year of publication;
- page number or numbers.

This is the skeleton. Now use it to examine any system you have in front of you by looking for the following kinds of variation:

- *Omissions*. Sometimes there are major limbs that become

detached (e.g. publisher's name, page number, p. before page number).

- *Additions.* Sometimes other bones are added on (e.g. the name of the editor of a book in which an article appears, the volume *and* number of a journal).

- *Order of assembly.* Sometimes the elements are sequenced one way (e.g. first name, given name, date, title, place) and sometimes another (e.g. given name, first name, title, place, date).

- *Punctuation.* Almost every time you look at a new system you will find the bones secured at the joints by different conventions of punctuation. Look in particular at the use and disposition of parentheses, commas, colons, semi-colons, fullstops, single quotation marks, double quotation marks and capital letters. You will rarely be able to predict with confidence how they operate in an unfamiliar system. The only rule that seems not to be variable is the one which says that the titles of books or other major works (not essays or journal articles) and the names of journals should be underlined.

- *Context.* In some disciplines one set of conventions might be used for references appearing in footnotes and another for references appearing in the bibliography at the end of the same essay.

- *Ordering of entries in the bibliography.* Most arts and social science disciplines order the bibliography or list of references alphabetically according to the author's family name in European and some other cultures. (Be aware that in some cultures quite the same distinction between 'family' and 'given' name does not apply.) Some science disciplines sequence the list by number allocated in the order in which the works are referred to in the text. Check this if one of your subjects is on the disciplinary borders.

- *Items to be included in the bibliography.* Some departments encourage you to list all your relevant reading in the bibliography; others view this practice with extreme disfavour, allowing you to list only those works you have referred to in the text of your essay. Do not 'pad' your bibliography unless you are sure this is permitted. Always ensure that any work referred to in your text is in fact included in the final list of references.

- *Title*. Some departments wish your final list to be called 'Bibliography', others 'References'. Respect this wish.
- *Annotations*. Sometimes you will be asked to annotate your bibliography – to write a few lines saying how and to what extent each item contributed to your essay. Do not annotate unless specifically instructed to.

Do not expect to feel comfortable with all these conventions immediately. Since they are rites, you will have to go through a period of preparation and initiation, a period in which you might feel rather uncertain of yourself. Most tutors will give you some time to master these things. They will, even so, begin to become impatient if you do not show attention to this detail and demonstrate progress from essay to essay. The point was made in chapter 1 that you should not spend so much effort on conforming to these conventions that other aspects of your thinking, reading and writing suffer. The fact remains, nevertheless, that well-written essays tend also to get the essentials of these conventions right.

Appendix 1

Writing book reviews

An essay, as we have seen, demands that you analyse arguments and evidence in order to decide on your best answer to the question raised by the topic. Fundamental to this answer is your argument and your evaluation. A book review requires you to perform the same tasks. Just as you begin your work on an essay by asking of your topic 'What is this question driving at?', so you begin work on a book review by asking 'What is this book driving at?' In everything we have had to say about reading we have stressed the importance of asking yourself constantly 'What is this author DOING?' This is the first question a book reviewer will ask. The reviewer will also ask two other questions: 'How well was it done?' and 'Was it worth doing?' Answering these questions involves assessing the book's contribution to the field of study.

If you feel diffident about your ability to give an authoritative assessment of the book's contribution to public *knowledge* in the subject, you nevertheless have a significant alternative open to you. This is to evaluate the author's contribution to your own *understanding* of the subject within the context of the other works you have read. Notice this last condition. You will not be able to assess any single work if you do not try to integrate it into what you already know.

Appendix 1

The broad procedures to adopt in working on a book review are therefore these:

1 Try to get a provisional idea of what the author is fundamentally trying to do in the book – what his or her major *motives* are. You can establish your 'first approximations' by looking at the jacket, the preface, the introduction or introductory chapter and the table of contents – more or less in that order. (Practised reviewers also commonly look through the bibliography at this stage.) Write down your provisional statement.

2 Try to write down a sketch of an 'opening paragraph' to an essay you might write on this subject, mentioning any other books that come to mind. (You might find it better to do this first.)

3 Go back to the book, looking again at the introductory matter and noting which of the chapters might seem especially interesting to you. *Read* the index in order to see which topics are included (noting any that come to mind which might be omitted), and assess by the entries and density of page references the emphasis given to particular subjects.

4 Browse through the book, concentrating on those chapters of particular interest or on the subjects which you know something about. As you do this, keep trying to establish the connections between the author's general motives and the more specific things he or she does. The kinds of thing to look for are set out in chapter 3 of this book. Make a few notes.

5 In the light of what you have done so far, make some revisions to what you have written down. This revision might well become the draft opening of your review.

6 Read the book properly from cover to cover taking notes as you go in the manner suggested in chapter 3.

7 Draft your review as you would an essay. Use much the same approach to the middle of the review as is set out in chapter 5. You will need to make many fewer references to other works, if any at all, than you would for an essay, for you will be concentrating on a critique of the book before you. In trying to assess how well the task has been performed by the author of your book, you will need to have some criteria in mind. These can be supplied by your reading of other works and by such appropriate general and specific criteria as are sketched out in chapter 9. While you are writing, keep the book under review beside you so that you can check your assertions.

8 If you have analysed the book in the manner suggested above, you should have been able to impose your own shape on the review. Resist the temptation to 'tell the story' according to the same sequence of ideas, chapters or events as the author uses.

9 Do not be afraid to comment on the way in which the book is written. If you found the language hard to understand, at least in part, give a few examples and try to interpret them (see chapter 3, section 7). With practice and experience you might be able to build up a way of discussing the success with which the author reconciles language with content.

10 References and a bibliography are appropriate to your review if you have made specific reference to other works in your text.

The processes of preparing a book review are set out above as stages or steps. Do not feel constrained to follow them slavishly if you find you can work better in another way – perhaps by combining some of those I have separated into one set of procedures. For example, you might well react so strongly to the author's language (either favourably or not) or to the author's treatment of a particular aspect of the subject somewhere in the middle of the book that you will choose to organise your work around that. Writing a review is the best way to make a book a part of yourself. Your review should try to reflect this.

Appendix 2

Sample analyses of essay topics

1 French

One critic has said: 'Truffaut is trying to establish connections between theatre and politics, between personal relationships and political involvement, between the idealism of the few and the pragmatism of the many.'

Do you think he succeeds in his aims? What verbal and visual means does he use to establish these connections?

1 The meanings of terms

Truffaut – a French film maker.

Idealism and pragmatism – check standard dictionary definitions of these terms as a start. For example, *The Concise Oxford Dictionary* has: *Idealism* – 'representation of things in ideal form'; *ideal* – 'answering to one's highest conception; . . . existing only in idea; visionary . . .'. *Pragmatism* – 'officiousness; pedantry . . . doctrine that estimates any assertion solely by its practical bearing upon human interests'.

Verbal and visual means – review the course so far and references given to get an idea about the categories of (a) verbal analysis and (b) visual analysis that are appropriate. No other problems with the understanding of terms.

2 Relationships of meaning between terms

How many questions are being asked? There seem to be two ('Do you think. . . ?' and 'What verbal and visual means. . . ?'). How can I reduce these to one fundamental question?

The fundamental question which requires my own evaluative answer is the first. The second question can be integrated into my answer to this by considering it as a set of reasons for this answer, for example Truffaut succeeds in his aims because he uses these visual means and these verbal means to good effect.

Here is the key: the three sets of connections listed in the topic are the 'aims'. The verbal and visual categories of analysis are the 'means'. Therefore I have to establish how well Truffaut realises his aims within the means specified. There are, on the surface, two sets of terms (or variables) to be related: aims and means.

NB. There is a third variable not mentioned in the topic. Which film (or films) are to be considered? If this is not clear from the course itself, a tutor should be consulted. We will assume just one film in what follows.

3 The shapes of some possible answers

3.1 All

In film X Truffaut succeeds completely in realising all three aims because he controls the verbal means (to be specified) and the visual means (to be specified) perfectly.

3.2 None

Truffaut fails entirely. In film X he manages to establish no clear connections between any of the three issues because his verbal and visual techniques do not work.

This seems to be an unlikely answer if only because the second question – 'What verbal and visual means does he use to establish these connections?' – assumes that there has been some success. If this case is to be argued, check first with the tutor because it changes the assumptions behind the questions.

3.3 *Some*

The fact that there are three 'aims' and two 'means' to be related gives an extremely large set of possible shapes for an answer. Here is just one fairly obvious approach:

> Truffaut succeeds well with respect to his first aim because he manages here to integrate both his visual and verbal techniques in order to establish the connections between theatre and politics. However, he is less successful in achieving his second and third aims because, although his visual effects work well (indicate how), the language of the film leaves unclear the precise nature of the connections between the personal and the political on the one hand, and between idealism and pragmatism on the other (indicate how).

The various permutations on this answer should be reasonably clear. But instead of focusing on the 'aims', an alternative approach might be to organise an answer around 'means'. This would possibly be more difficult in certain respects, but is nevertheless possible. For example:

> Truffaut is a better film-maker than he is a dramatist. Those connections that lend themselves particularly to visual images are handled better than those which rely more especially on words. The means by which he establishes the connections between more concrete things – theatre and politics, the personal and the political – are achieved well. Idealism and pragmatism are abstractions harder to realise in visual images; and this is where Truffaut is less successful. His language never sufficiently distinguishes between what might just as well be the self-consciously expressed pragmatism of the few and the inadequately articulated idealism of the many.

Having thought about such possibilities as these, I should need to formulate one of them and put it to the test of further reading and observation.

2 Physical geography

Uplift and mountain building are of fundamental importance to the origin of landforms. Discuss some of the ideas proposed to account for the existence of mountains, paying particular attention to those which involve the theory of plate tectonics.

Illustrate your answer where possible with reference to Australia, New Zealand and Papua New Guinea.

1 The meanings of terms

From John B. Whittow's *Penguin Dictionary of Physical Geography* (London, 1984) comes this information:

Uplift – movement of the crustal rocks '*en masse* in a vertical or radial direction' at a continental scale.

Mountain building – folding, faulting and thrusting 'during which sediments are buckled and deformed'. Unlike uplift, this is tangential to the earth rather than vertical or radial.

Plate tectonics – the theory, developed in the 1960s, that the earth's crust is constructed of seven major and twelve smaller plates, which are moved about by large-scale thermal convection currents.

2 Relationships of meaning between terms

Can uplift and mountain building be considered synonymous for the purposes of this essay? Probably not – see definitions above.

Establish what other 'ideas' besides the plate tectonics theory try to account for mountain building.

Relate the theories ('ideas') to the evidence from Australia, New Zealand and New Guinea. Relate it also to some evidence *not* from this region. Which idea (or combination of ideas) does this evidence give strongest support to?

3 Shapes of some possible answers

3.1 All

Of the various ideas put forward to account for the existence of mountains, plate tectonics has no rival. The evidence from the study of both uplift and mountain building in Australia, New Zealand and New Guinea gives complete support to that from elsewhere in confirming the plate tectonic hypothesis. The reasons are . . .

3.2 *None*

The evidence from the study of both uplift and mountain building in Australia, New Zealand and New Guinea, like that from elsewhere, offers no support to the ideas of plate tectonics. The things that this theory cannot explain are . . . It is other ideas, namely. . . , that can explain these phenomena.

3.3 *Some*

There are five fairly clear variables to be considered in thinking of possible shapes for a discussion of this topic – plate tectonic theory; other theories; uplift and mountain building; the evidence from Australia, New Zealand and New Guinea (this is a complex variable which it might be possible to break down into a number of 'subvariables', since the geological information on these three countries might not all point to the same conclusions); evidence from other parts of the world. Therefore, like the topic from French considered above, there will be many ways in which the variables can, in principle, be combined. Here is just one example of a possible shape for the answer:

Of the ? main theories which attempt to account for uplift and mountain building, plate tectonics is well supported by much of the evidence from Australia, New Zealand and New Guinea. Better than any other idea, plate tectonics explains folding and faulting in mountain formation. However, there are certain significant features of uplift in parts of this region (particularly . . .) which p.t. can account for no better than – and, in certain instances, not quite as well as – the older ideas of . . . There appears to be uplift in other parts of the world which similarly poses difficulties for the p.t. theory. The problem is therefore how to reconcile the inconsistencies between p.t. and other ideas using the evidence on uplift we now have.

3 Political economy

How do commodity markets affect the efficiency of economic planning in the Third World?

1 Meanings of terms

Commodity markets – markets for the types of primary commodity typically produced by Third World countries, for example coffee, tea, copra, sisal, rice, wheat, minerals, coal, oil. Assume that these markets are international (not merely domestic) and that the commodities are a major source of foreign hard-currency earnings.

2 Relationships of meaning between terms

The question asks how. Therefore it will be necessary to establish the means or the ways in which the terms are to be related. There are three terms to be related – commodity markets, efficiency of economic planning, Third World countries. At least the first and last of these are potentially complex terms: some commodity markets might be different from others; the planning circumstances might vary considerably between different Third World countries. It might be possible to tackle this essay by generalising about Third World countries as a whole (i.e. by treating them as a simple term). But since not all such countries produce the same commodities, treating them together might in turn depend in part on whether all relevant commodity markets behave similarly, which they may not (e.g. presence or absence of cartels, bilateral trade agreements, elasticity of demand for certain commodities). Perhaps Third World countries should be subclassified according to the main types of market in which they engage.

Efficiency of economic planning – necessary to find out what criteria or indices of efficiency might be appropriate. Some provisional ones might be: ability to forecast within reasonable limits production levels over a typical five-year plan; ability to forecast earnings of foreign exchange in volatile markets; ability to forecast ratio of earnings from commodities to price movements of imported capital goods; ability to forecast fluctuations in interest rates on borrowings. What criteria of efficient planning might *not* be affected by commodity markets? Should the *ceteris paribus* clause (other things being equal) be invoked to hold these constant?

3 The shape of a possible answer

'All' and 'none' answers are inappropriate to a how question. Rather, this kind of question requires a decision on which of the ways or means are the most important, and which the less important:

> The ways in which commodity markets affect the efficiency of economic planning in Third World countries will depend upon a number of factors, chief among which are the nature of the commodities themselves and the conditions which determine the behaviour of the market. Planning efficiency in any Third World country is largely dependent (along with other things which we shall not examine) on the ability to forecast the prices the commodities will fetch in the international market. If there are ways in which price fluctuations can be minimised, economic planning can be reasonably efficient. But this happens with relatively few commodities. Many Third World commodity producers are at the mercy not only of unforeseeable fluctuations in both supply and demand but also of interest rates on borrowings. By contrast, they can be fairly sure about continuing and predictable price rises in the capital goods that need to be imported in order to develop the economy. It is therefore the difficulty of relating earnings from commodities to interest repayments rather than to the prices of capital imports that constitutes the main barrier to efficient planning in most Third World economies.

Remember that the proposals above are not answers to the questions contained in these essay topics. They are merely possible shapes for an answer that I have produced 'off the top of my head'. Where I have lacked the information or an insight into what to say, I have simply left three dots. Where I have filled in these things (as in the example on commodity markets), I have merely taken a somewhat blind stab at what might turn out to be quite inadequate statements. Only consultation of sources can reveal the adequacy (or inadequacy) of these attempts.

Appendix 3

A revised manuscript

INSERT ①

~~In The Tempest,~~ /ʀeason is set against 'fury' and
nurture against nature. / INSERT ② ~~But the duke~~ Prospero, the exiled Duke of Milan, though the dominant, force in the play, is not
~~the~~ a perfect exemplar of the providential power of
reason and nurture, any more than his slave /Caliban is a savage

ruled solely by fury and unregenerate nature.
Prospero's/ white magical Art, despite the contrasts he/ himself draws
with the/ black magic of 'the foul witch Sycorax', is not a

humane kind of learning; for otherwise he would have
His Art is alchemical and redolent of the philosopher's stone.
no cause to renounce it at the end of the play./ Nor

is it true, as Prospero says of Caliban, that ~~he~~ the slave is 'A

devil, a born devil, on whose nature / Nurture can
(IV, i, 188-9)
never stick'/. Caliban does learn, arguably even more

237

than Prospero, inasmuch as at the end of the play he resolves ~~says~~ 'I'll be wise hereafter,/And seek for grace' ⊙ *This is a resolution* which finds no echo in anything Prospero promises ~~says~~. [If we

are to look for a touchstone to knowledge in <u>The Tempest</u>, it will be found in *Prospero's daughter* Miranda, in whom nature

and nurture, reason and passion are perfectly mixed. INSERT ④ *But at the end of it all, she* ~~Miranda~~ does not *actually* 'know' very much ~~at all~~ about the world, *the prince* on first seeing Ferdinand she thinks him,

without any hint of metaphor, a spirit, 'a thing divine'. *The kind of learning* ~~What~~ she *does* displays is *a quality* ~~something~~ *vastly* more *than anything her father has actually taught her—* important, a depth of *human* understanding or sympathy.

Prospero's learning seems to be of two quite distinct kinds. Neither *proves to be* ~~is~~ admirable. In recounting

the story of how he was dispossessed of his dukedom,

he boasts to Miranda how

                 being so reputed

In dignity, and for the liberal Arts

Without a parallel; those being all my study,

The government I cast upon my brother,

> And to my state grew stranger, being transported

> And rapt in secret studies. (I,ii,72-7)

Prospero's studies were ~~of~~ _in_ the seven ~~traditional~~ _Conventional_
liberal arts, and through absorption in them/ _he_ forfeited
his power in the state. A duke, _he now realises,_ cannot be a pure
scholar or theoretician. ⌃These liberal ~~studies were~~ _arts he then replaces with th_
less conventional
~~not the~~ magical Art that he practise _s_ on the island.
(⌃The studies were 'secret' only in the sense that they
were private and recondite.) This latter/ _is a_ 'so potent
that he makes use of
Art' ~~was studied~~ solely for the power it bestowe _s_ on

an egocentric Prospero to do violence to nature ('I

INSERT ⑤ (V,i,41ff)⊙ _Learning of this kind is_
have bedimm'd / The noontide sun') ~~and to effect his~~
effected solely for _those who toppled him from his dukedom._ _too,_
/revenge on ~~other people~~ We notice, /that the volumes

he once _d_ _have_ _whittled down to_
that ~~Prospero~~ prize _s_ 'above my dukedom'/ become/ a

Prospero _as a manual_
single 'book' (III,i,94;V,i,57), which ~~the~~ consults/ to
experimental _with nature and human beings. This handbook_
further his/ project /~~and which~~ he promises to drown

only when he can be sure that he will no longer have

book is Stephano's
to rely on it. ~~The book to~~ Prospero _'s_ ~~is little more~~

~~than the~~ bottle. ~~to the drunken butler Stephano~~

239

Appendix 3

This is something Caliban learns. He knows better than the drunken butler Stephano and the equally drunken jester Trinculo that the rebellion against Prospero to dispossess him of the island can only succeed if first they burn the master's books. Without them, Caliban has realised, Prospero is 'but a sot, as I am, nor hath not / One spirit to command' (III, ii, 90-1). Shakespeare draws a clear parallel between the effect of Stephano's 'celestial liquor' on Caliban and the effect of Prospero's charms – 'the ignorant fumes that mantle / Their clearer reason' (V, i, 67-8) – on the usurpers the duke wishes to master. The sense of power conferred by the butt of sack is, of course, illusory; but so is that of Prospero's Art. Both turn ordinary mortals into 'masters', a word used to suggest at once authority and lack of control constantly throughout the play. True learning is not a matter of attaining mastery over nature, over other people or even, through the use of cool reason, over oneself. It is Gonzalo who wishes this insight to be set down 'With gold on lasting pillars':

in one voyage

Did Claribel her husband find at Tunis,

And Ferdinand, her brother, found a wife

Where he himself was lost, Prospero his dukedom

In a poor isle, and all of us ourselves

When no man was his own. (V,i, 208-13)

Index

Index

Index

Index

Index

Index

'the' + abstract noun, 177
theories, 8, 27, 30, 191
THEORISING, *see* analysis, modes of
'therefore', 168
thesaurus, 109
thinking, 12, 21–51 *passim*
    and language, 109, 175–6, 205, 210
time, efficient use of, 22, 23
time and tense, 150–3
timetables, 4, 11
'to', 177
    vs 'from', 156
    vs 'with', 203
topic paragraph, 121
topic sentence, *see* main point
tutor, consultation of, 14, 26, 40, 163,
    231, 232
tutors' comments, 14, 112, 113–14, 117,
    122, 129, 162–3, 186
tutors' expectations, 2–3, 7, 8, 13, 25,
    149, 156, 158, 205, 226

underlining, 179–81
'understand', 148
understanding, 12, 158–9, 227
    and grammar, 162
'uninterested' vs 'disinterested', 155–6
unity, *see* coherence

validity, 188, 189
verbless sentences, 165–7
verbs
    auxiliary ('be', 'have' and modals),
        165
    finite and non-finite, 164–7, 170, 175
    modal, 165
    of enquiry, perception and analysis,
        146–8, 155–8, 170, 173
    substitute ('be', 'do', 'happen'), 166

vocabulary
    disciplinary differences, 37, 178–9,
        189, 191
    of academic enquiry, 181
    patterning of, 209–10, 213–14
    technical, 221; *see also* jargon

'we', use of, 143–6, 148, 152, 154, 220
weighting criteria, 198, 200
Weldon, T. D., 81–2
'whereas', 168, 169, 202, 220
'which' clause, 192, 196–7, 220
Whittow, John B., 233
Wilding, John M., 60
'will'– 'would', 165
'wish', 158
'with', 203
word limits, 109–10, 113, 121, 126–7
words
    choice of, 2, 11
    confusion with things, 179–83
    elusive, 109
    see also repetition of words;
        substitution of words;
        vocabulary
'writer's block', 3–7, 10, 27, 108–9
    see also grinding to a halt
writing
    and knowledge, 1–2
    and thinking, 22–3, 107
    as debate, 3, 66, 99–104
    elements of, 2–3, 1–18 *passim*
    problems of, 107–11

Yeats, W. B., 143
'yes, but' discussion, 72–3, 99–100
    see also motives, conceding
'you', use of, 220
    see also reader, addressing the